THE GREAT HEDGE
OF INDIA

THE
GREAT HEDGE
OF INDIA

ROY MOXHAM

Constable • London

Constable Publishers
3 The Lanchesters
162 Fulham Palace Road
London W6 9ER
www.constablerobinson.com

First published in the UK by Constable,
an imprint of Constable & Robinson Ltd 2001

A copy of the British Library Cataloguing in
Publication data is available from the British Library

ISBN 1-84119-260-0

Printed and bound in the EU

Contents

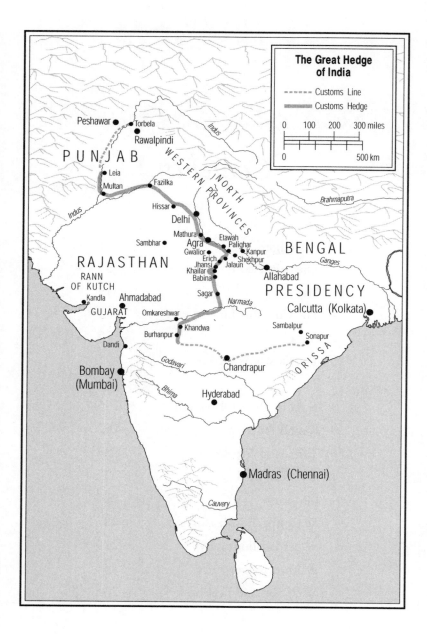

The Great Hedge
of India

- - - - - Customs Line
━━━━━ Customs Hedge

0   100   200   300 miles

0   500 km

Peshawar
Torbela
Rawalpindi
Indus

PUNJAB
WESTERN
Leia
Multan   Fazilka
NORTH PROVINCES
Brahmaputra

Indus   Hissar
Delhi
Mathura   Etawah
Sambhar   Agra   Palighar
Gwalior   Kanpur   BENGAL
RAJASTHAN   Erich   Shekhpur   *Ganges*
Jhansi   Jalaun
RANN   Khailar
OF KUTCH   Babina   Allahabad
Kandla   Sagar   PRESIDENCY
Ahmadabad   *Narmada*
GUJARAT   Omkareshwar   Calcutta (Kolkata)
Khandwa   Sambalpur
Dandi   Burhanpur   Sonapur
Godavari   Chandrapur   ORISSA
Bombay
(Mumbai)   *Bhima*   Hyderabad

Madras (Chennai)

Cauvery

ONE

A Hedge?

In populated parts of the country, where smuggling is rife,
the men are active in preventing the passage of contraband
goods by a barrier which, in its most perfect form, is
utterly impassable to man or beast and all the outlets
through which are guarded.

ALLAN OCTAVIAN HUME, Commissioner of Inland Customs

O n the corner of Charing Cross Road and Lichfield Street, right in the centre of London, there is a second-hand bookshop – Quinto. Its haphazard collections, often dilapidated, rarely contain anything grand. The books are cheap. A bargain is always a possibility. I first went to India in 1992, and have returned every year. As I became more interested in the country's culture and history, I started to acquire a few books. Some were new; some second-hand. I kept away from expensive antiquarian shops. Nevertheless, I occasionally found quite rare items. Quinto was a favourite haunt.

It was there, late in 1995, that I paid £25 for *Rambles and Recollections of an Indian Official,* by Major-General Sir W. H.

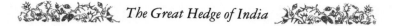

Sleeman KCB. For a book published in 1893, and containing many lending date-stamps from Cheltenham Public Library, its two olive-green cloth volumes were in good condition. It was a lot of money for me – more than I had ever spent on a second-hand book before – but I liked the title. It was fortunate that I had neither the money, nor inclination, to buy first editions. It had always struck me as a nonsense that a first edition should be more prized than a later edition, with the errors removed and the text expanded.

Sleeman's book was a fascinating account of travels through India in the last decades of the Honourable East India Company's rule. It told of the author's trek across central India, leading a tour of inspection, at the head of a huge caravan of elephants and horses. There were eyewitness accounts of rajas and ranies, of famines and battles, of religious ceremonies and widow burning, of bandits, poisoners and witchcraft. There was also a chapter on 'Transit duties in India – mode of collecting them', which dwelt on the 'insolence and rapacity of these customs house officers', as they extracted bribes. These reflections were made as the caravan passed through a customs post at Horal, between Delhi and Agra. It seemed that goods were taxed as they entered 'British' India from the Princely States to the west. It had never occurred to me before that customs duties had been levied, hundreds of miles from the coast, in the heart of India.

It was a quite interesting chapter. What really caught my

eye, however, was a footnote. This had been appended to the
original edition by an editor from the Indian Civil Service,
quoting another Indian civil servant, Lytton Strachey's father,
Sir John Strachey:

> To secure the levy of a duty on salt . . . there grew up
> gradually a monstrous system, to which it would be
> almost impossible to find a parallel in any tolerably
> civilised country. A Customs line was established which
> stretched across the whole of India, which in 1869
> extended from the Indus to the Mahanadi in Madras, a
> distance of 2,300 miles; and it was guarded by nearly
> 12,000 men . . . It would have stretched from London to
> Constantinople . . . It consisted principally of an
> immense impenetrable hedge of thorny trees and
> bushes.

A hedge? It seemed unlikely. I checked the usual histories
of India, and found no reference to it. Surely, with the Salt Tax
being such an important issue right up to independence, this
was emotive history. This was a hedge of massive proportions;
a hedge that would have existed in the time of living people's
grandparents. For such a hedge to have been forgotten seemed
unthinkable. Perhaps Strachey had got it wrong. Perhaps he
had been misquoted.

By a lucky coincidence, I had just started work as conservator of the University of London Library. For the first few
months I was very busy, with no time to pursue personal

interests. Also, not being a librarian, it took some time to master even the basics of the idiosyncratic cataloguing system. I checked the computer catalogue, but found nothing. It was April 1996 when I eventually found, in the old-fashioned card catalogue, Strachey's book, written jointly with his brother Richard, *The Finances and Public Works of India, 1869–1881*. It sounded comprehensive and trust-worthy.

And so it turned out, in so far as the facts of construction were concerned. On social and political matters it was more suspect – justifying the Salt Tax as enlightened imperialism, as it similarly sought to justify the production of opium destined for China. The chapter on the Salt Tax confirmed the details quoted in the footnote to Sleeman's book. Apart from a reference to there being 1,720 guard-posts, and to a Mr Grant Duff who had seen the hedge and said that it could be compared to nothing else in the world except the Great Wall of China, there was little further information. In particular, there were no details of the precise location of the hedge. It did, however, refer to a report by the Commissioner of Inland Customs for 1869–70. This was my next lead. My colleagues told me that I was most likely to find the report in the India Office Records.

The India Office Records, awaiting transfer to the new British Library, were in a dreary building on Blackfriars Road. Fortunately it was open on Saturday mornings, and only twenty minutes' walk from my flat, so I was able to make frequent visits. It was easy to obtain a reader's pass.

The India Office Records contained the archives of the East India Company, which ruled India until 1858, and those of the India Office, which ruled it from then to independence in 1947. There was a mass of other related material. The archive occupied nine miles of shelving. There were also 70,000 official publications, relating to India before independence, and 70,000 maps.

Inside, the reading room was surprisingly attractive – solid wooden cabinets and tables, and about a hundred readers' chairs; a thick, richly coloured carpet; the wooden armchair of the Chairmen of the East India Company. The staff were helpful, the finding instructions clear, and I soon had on my desk the Annual Report of the India Inland Customs Department for 1869–70. It was full of information about the hedge. Over succeeding Saturdays I read all the other available Annual Reports in the series – starting in 1867 and ending in 1878.

The first reports detailed a massive reorganisation of the Customs Line. A series of separate unconnected sections had been amalgamated into one continuous line. That had resulted in some spurs, often hundreds of miles long, being made redundant. (One such separate spur was left intact – running 280 miles west from the Rann of Kutch.) Gaps between the old lines had been filled in, and new extensions carried the line south and east, from its origin in the Himalayas. It followed the Indus River, down through what is now Pakistan; skirted Delhi, then went on to Agra, Jhansi, Hoshangabad, Khandwa, Chandrapur, and Raipur; to end on the Mahanadi River, in what is now the Indian State of Orissa. It was one line, 2,504 miles long.

Other Annual Reports gave additional information. There was even a rough map. In less populated parts of the country, and to the east, the Customs Line merely had the occasional marker and was supervised by widely spread-out men. In other areas it was completely different. The Commissioner wrote:

> In populated parts of the country, where smuggling is rife, the men are active in preventing the passage of contraband goods by a barrier which, in its most perfect form, is utterly impassable to man or beast, and all the outlets through which are guarded.
>
> As a rule, the barrier is a hedge, green or dry, but in some places where bare rocks preclude the possibility of raising a green hedge, and the absence of vegetation in the neighbourhood deprives us of the materials, we have begun to construct stone walls.
>
> The dry hedge is chiefly composed of masses of the dwarf Indian plum, supported and strengthened by stakes firmly driven into the ground. Portions of the barrier thus constructed, in locations where the 'jhurberry' is plentiful, exceed in strength and size even the perfect live hedges. But in most places material is procured with more or less difficulty, and at a cost of enormous labour: white ants and jungle fires perpetually destroy the dry hedge, at which our work is ceaseless; while storm and whirlwinds, especially in the sandy

plain of the Punjab, carry away whole furlongs, and even occasionally, miles, of it in an hour.

In its most perfect form the hedge is a live one, from ten to fourteen feet in height, and six to twelve feet thick, composed of closely clipped thorny trees and shrubs, amongst which the babool (accacia catecha), the Indian plum (zizyphues jujuba), the carounda (carissa curonda), the prickly pear (opuntia, three species), and the thuer (euphorbia, several species) are, according to salt and climate, the most numerous, with which a thorny creeper (guilandina bondue) is constantly inter-mingled.

So here was the hedge, described in minute detail, even down to the plants that made it. It had been abandoned and forgotten. Surely, I thought, some fragments, some memories, must remain. Suddenly, on a whim, and because I was planning a trip to India, I decided to look for them. I thought it might be fun to uncover the traces of such an eccentric enterprise; of such a quintessentially British folly.

I had already arranged to go to India in October for a month. I intended to see some of the smaller old towns in south Rajasthan, to visit a friend in Delhi, and if possible stay in an

Indian village for a while. I had been taking classes in Hindi, and was anxious to get some real practice.

Didi, my friend in Delhi, came from a village in Uttar Pradesh, between Kanpur and Jhansi, and we had already discussed the possibility of my staying with her family there. The rough map I had found in the Annual Report showed the hedge as passing fairly close to the village. It seemed a fortuitous coincidence. What I now needed was an accurate large-scale map of the Customs Hedge.

Many of the maps in the India Office records dated from before the great re-routing of the Customs Line in 1869. Many others dated from after it was abandoned in 1879. Some of the earlier maps might show the whereabouts of the unaltered sections of the line, and some of the later maps might show traces of the defunct hedge. I decided, however, to start with the period 1869–79.

On succeeding Saturdays, working from the nineteenth-century catalogue, I ordered up dozens of maps. It was a frustrating business. The dates on many of the maps were different to those listed in the catalogue – invariably later editions with no sign of the Customs Hedge. Other maps, which looked hopeful, had been scored through in the catalogue, with annotations such as 'Transferred to India', or 'Sent to the War Office'. Goodness only knows where they had finally ended up. Other maps were of too small a scale, covered the wrong areas, or were missing.

It was mid-September – and I was flying out to India on the 29th – before I found anything useful. A map of the 'North

West Provinces', printed in Calcutta in 1874, had a line running across it which might have been the hedge. Unfortunately, the map was thirty-two miles to the inch, and it had no key. Nevertheless, there was a clear black line, which tallied with the map and descriptions in the Annual Reports. Also – and this seemed the strongest reason for believing it was indeed the hedge – there were, at strategic intervals, what looked like symbols of forts. It did cross my mind that I might be looking at an old territorial boundary (and, of course, the hedge was likely to follow the same route), but it seemed more likely that it was the line of the Customs Hedge. Photocopying was not allowed, so I copied out by hand the important details. I noted the villages it ran through. One, Jalaun, gave its name to the district in which my friend's village lay.

I felt confident that I would find some remnants of the Customs Hedge. I was even hopeful that, given the proximity of the hedge to the village, some old people might have been told about it in their childhood.

I flew into Delhi at the end of September 1996. It was my fifth journey to India in as many years, and I experienced none of the trepidation I had felt on my first trip. That had been an overpowering and frightening experience. For many years friends had been urging me to go to India. 'You'll love it!' they said. I had not been so sure. As a young man I had spent several years in eastern Africa. That I had loved. The vast open spaces of Africa had made a strong impression on me, and I had always seen them as the antithesis of an over-crowded India. Some newsreel footage I had seen of the Calcutta slums had stuck in my memory. Nevertheless, the continual enthusing of friends and acquaintances who knew India had its effect. When I read an article in a Sunday newspaper supplement by Norman Lewis – a writer I much admired – likening parts of southern India to my beloved east African coast, I decided to take the risk and go. I flew into Bombay.

Inside the airport terminus it was relatively quiet. For security reasons only staff and passengers could gain access; air-conditioning made it cool. I stepped out into a different world. The air was no longer cold and clinical, but warm and heavy. It had a scent that was difficult to place – perhaps a mix of tropical seas and stale excrement. I stood for a moment adjusting to the brilliant light. Then I was engulfed in a maelstrom of auto-rickshaw drivers desperate for my custom. They crowded close, shouting and gesticulating, making grabs for my baggage. I tightened my grasp on the handles.

'No! No!' I said. 'I'm looking for the airport bus into town.'

'They're on strike,' a driver said.

I looked at him closely. He was more respectable-looking than the others – clean-shaven, and with neatly pressed shirt and trousers.

'On strike? Are you sure?'

'Oh, yes, there's been no buses for over a week now.'

'Is that true?' I asked the others, who were still pressed around.

'Yes. Yes. Yes,' they replied as one.

'How much?'

'By the meter, sahib. Come.'

He eased my fingers off the bag, hoisted it up high, and led me to his battered yellow three-wheeled auto-rickshaw. The windscreen was almost totally obscured by paintings of Hindu gods and goddesses. He kicked the two-stroke engine into life and we set off down the Bombay highway. After a few minutes, however, we swung off on to a rutted narrow track.

'Where are you going!' I exclaimed, having visions of being kidnapped and robbed, with no one knowing my whereabouts.

'No problem,' the driver said, and laughed. 'Short-cut.'

A minute later we entered a city built of tin and hessian — tin from beaten oil-drums, hessian from worn-out sacks. Thousands upon thousands of makeshift huts, lopsided and ramshackle, housed large families in small single rooms. Children defecated in the open. Their excrement ran towards the lower level of the track we were on, to join the rest of the puddled sewage. We ploughed through the evil sludge. A litter of foraging black pigs ran away squealing. The smell hit me, and I gagged.

From time to time, we slowed to negotiate a pothole or a dirty pool of unknown depth. That was a signal for us to be besieged by begging children, or the maimed. Emaciated fingers and leprous stumps clawed at my arms. How much longer, I thought, how much longer in this awful place. I glanced at the meter. It was still on zero.

I found out later that the airport buses were not on strike, and that I had traversed the largest slum in the whole of Asia. Bombay, with perhaps 14,000,000 people, has created a slum much larger and more horrific than any in Calcutta. Four million people battle for survival with no sanitary facilities. The amazing thing is that, beyond the beggars and the urchins, the inhabitants go about their lives with so much good humour and dignity. Men joked as they washed themselves in muddy pools; women in tattered saris combed through piles of rubbish with a smile.

The centre of Bombay where, after a massive argument over the fare, the driver eventually dropped me off at my hotel, was actually rather pleasant. Although the air was still not clean, the noxious smell was much diluted. The streets had flowering trees. For me, however, my first impressions were impossible to eradicate. I knew I was being rather unfair on Bombay, and had not given it a proper chance. Some of my friends much preferred Bombay to Delhi or Calcutta, but not me. All I wanted to do was leave, and quickly.

Fortunately, I was able obtain a ticket to go by train next day to Mysore. The journey, 850 miles south, took exactly 24 hours, and I arrived in the middle of the evening. The carriage was air-conditioned, so I had been insulated from any smell outside. I stepped out to discover the scent of Mysore – jasmine. Everywhere in Mysore you could smell it. The women braided it into their hair. The pavements were full of jasmine stalls. I breathed in deeply. It was wonderful.

On the way to my hotel I saw that in the streets there was none of the frenetic hustle of Bombay. The auto-rickshaw passed close to the palace. The grounds were open and full of promenading couples and families. The palace itself, and all the surrounding walls, were bedecked with many thousands of lights, so that it all looked like a picture in a book of fairy tales. I knew that I was going to like Mysore a lot. And like India too.

Four years later, I thought of myself as an old India hand. It was good to be returning to Delhi, a city that, despite the congestion and pollution, I revered. History is everywhere in Delhi. I loved to visit the remains of the old cities within the present boundaries; to discover forgotten tombs and mansions. This time, however, I wanted to depart as soon as possible for Jalaun District – to visit my friend's village, and to look for any remnants of the Customs Hedge. It was mid-October, however, before I was able to arrange this. Didi insisted that I must be accompanied by one of her male relatives, and they were all busy until then. I looked around Delhi and made a tour of Rajasthan, and then returned to Delhi to meet up with my escort. Didi's mother was also to travel with us to the village.

We took the Shatabdi Express from Delhi to Kanpur. This was the fastest train in India. We left New Delhi at six-twenty in the morning and were in Kanpur, 280 miles south-east, at ten past eleven. It was not an enjoyable journey. The double-glazing which sealed in the over-chilled air made it too cloudy to view the countryside and there were too many businessmen talking noisily into their mobile phones. Someone sitting behind us loudly compared the perfectly adequate complimentary breakfast unfavourably with that he had recently eaten on British Airways. My companions looked bemused. This was the first time they had travelled on such a luxury train.

Moola, Didi's mother, sat cross-legged on the comfortable blue armchair, wrapped in a blanket. Slight, and immensely dignified, she could deal with any situation. Having spent most of her life in one tiny village, she had taken her daughter's move to the city, and her own visits there – and in India the difference between the urban and rural areas was huge – calmly in her stride. Occasionally she shot me a reassuring smile.

Santosh, Didi's twenty-one-year-old nephew and Moola's grandson, looked less comfortable. He was overawed by the brash businessmen. He lived in Gwalior and had just finishing schooling there. He flicked through the free newspapers. However, on this expensive train they were all in English, a language he did not know. I had met Santosh on a previous trip, when he had been helpful to me in encounters with Indian bureaucracy. His aunt had summoned him to Delhi, to take his grandmother and me to the village, and then to help me search for the hedge. He was small and neat, extraordinarily helpful, and always cheerful.

From Kanpur we had to backtrack west. As the crow flew, it was only about twenty-five miles to the village, but the route was devious. We had left on the early express train to ensure we reached there before nightfall. First, we had to take a train to Kalpi. That was very different to the Shatabdi Express. It was the lowest class of train, with uncomfortable wooden seats. It had commenced its journey in Lucknow, and was full. We perched on our luggage, deep in litter, until seats gradually became available. There was a continual stream of vendors – tea, cold drinks, paper cones of spiced peanuts, and *samosas*. Blind and disfigured beggars solicited alms – mostly without much luck. More success came to a transvestite, who, in garish sari and smudged lipstick, seemed to get contributions from almost everyone. I resisted, until outrageous flirting gestures accompanied by loud kissing noises forced me to pay him off too.

On the bench opposite, a young woman read with unfaltering concentration. Her somewhat battered book had an untitled brown paper wrapper. Slowly I deciphered the title on top of the pages – it was Shakespeare's *Julius Caesar*. I opened up a conversation with her father – an agricultural officer, and the only remotely smartly dressed man on the train – who sat next to her, and then talked to her about Shakespeare. She was a chemistry student, but was re-reading all of Shakespeare, because 'I like him so much'. She was fascinated to learn that I came from near Stratford-upon-Avon. I spent the rest of the journey answering questions about life in Shakespeare's birthplace.

15

From Kalpi we had to go by road. It was some distance from the railway to the bus station, so we hailed an auto-rickshaw. We had hardly crushed into the narrow seats, when a policeman arrived. What, he wanted to know, were two ordinary Indians doing with a foreigner? We fitted none of the usual categories – a businessman with clients; a tourist with guides. Was I doing something not covered by my tourist visa? Was I being abducted? It was some time before I could persuade him that I was indeed, if somewhat improbably, a friend of the family. As we left, Moola and Santosh told me he had been looking for a bribe.

No buses went the entire way. The best option was a *tempo* to Mangrol, three miles before our village. The *tempo* was already waiting to go, and fully loaded. A fearsome three-wheeler, quite unlike the dainty auto-rickshaws, its rough metal body was heavily scratched and battered. The roof was festooned with baggage, sacks of grain, and children. As we looked inside, innumerable women drew the edge of their saris across their faces.

There was a cry from behind. Someone had recognised Moola, and we were being invited to tea. I demurred, for it was already three o'clock, and I was anxious to get to the village by dark. I was assured the *tempo* would wait for us. Refusal was impossible. We sat on the carpeted floor of an open cloth store, sipping milky tea out of small glasses. There were about a dozen men. Several more slipped in to join us. *Samosas* arrived. With my hesitant Hindi, and their smatterings of English, we chatted. More tea arrived. I explained that I did not wish to miss the *tempo*'s departure.

16

'How can you?' the shopkeeper asked, gesturing to a man who stood behind drinking tea, 'that is your driver. And,' he continued triumphantly, putting a hand on the shoulder of the man seated next to him, 'this is the owner!'

Everyone laughed and more tea appeared.

We crammed ourselves into the *tempo*. My knee was hard against the dashboard-mounted gear lever; Moola had been absorbed into the back compartment; Santosh was on the roof. The large low-geared two-stroke engine chugged noisily as we left the little town. We eased our way along rutted potholed roads.

I looked out across the flat plains of Uttar Pradesh. Everywhere was cultivated. Fields were being ploughed with tractors or oxen. Dense thickets of unharvested maize and sugar cane stood out like green walls. Feathery rushes marked the edges of irrigation canals. Muslim graves of brilliant white, and Hindu shrines topped with red flags, spotted the landscape. The *tempo* went faster as we dropped people off, but the sun had already set when we arrived outside Mangrol. The light was going fast, and we were preparing to walk the final stretch with our baggage, when the only tractor in Mangrol arrived back from the fields. For a few rupees the driver agreed to take us the three miles to the village. It was fortunate he had lights, for it was dark when we arrived.

The tiny house had no electricity. Moola's daughter, Ramkali, and her two children, Mohan and Nanani, greeted us. Soon we were eating *chapatis* and vegetables, under amazingly clear and large stars, and a vast Milky Way. There was no room for all of us inside the house, so Santosh and I made up our beds on the two *charpoys* out on the open veranda. A water buffalo tethered below breathed heavily. I was soon asleep.

The village of Shekhpur lay close to the Yamuna. Looking out from the house, over a few huts and across the fields, the river glistened between steep banks about three-quarters of a mile away. Although the Yamuna was now low, it was nevertheless several hundred yards wide. The month before we arrived, the river had flooded – the biggest flood in living memory – right up to the house, and over the dwellings below. Everyone was delighted, for it had laid fertile silt over the exhausted earth.

Although there was a slight incline down to the bank of the river, the general impression was of flatness. On the other sides of the village the land was flat too. Most of the fields were being prepared for planting, and were a bare grey-brown. There were no tractors in the village. All day the landscape was dotted with pairs of oxen. They were of the classic Indian breed, small and thin, with brown patches on the head and legs, but with very pale, almost white, bodies. They pulled single-furrow wooden ploughs, or heavy wooden beams that served as clod-breaking harrows. Farmers guided them from behind. Occasionally, a small patch of sugar cane or millet greened the view. Here and there were solitary trees.

18

In the flat landscape, these higher growths helped block off any sight of nearby villages. This gave a feeling of extraordinary isolation and, although I knew that this plain was one of the most heavily populated areas of India, I felt peculiarly detached from anywhere beyond the village.

The village itself had perhaps a hundred houses, which were closely packed in short rows, and separated by narrow rutted lanes. Many were not much more than huts. Nothing rose above two storeys, and roofs and ceilings were low, so that the buildings had little height. Maybe that, and the numerous shade trees, also helped explain the invisibility of the surrounding villages. Some of the roofs had crude curved tiles, but most were of coarse thatch. Some of the walls were of mud, but most were of rough brick. There was a small yard in front of nearly all of the dwellings, which was usually home to a tethered cow, or water buffalo, or a few goats. These nibbled away any greenery. Plate-sized mounds of dung, moulded by hand, dried out on the walls or roofs, or were piled in the yard. The smell of burning dung, not unpleasant, was always in the air. The overall colour of the village was that of the earth. Very occasionally an effort had been made to decorate the exterior of a house – some white plaster; some niches for lamps; even a latticed floor pattern drawn with white flour – but there was no colour.

The colour was provided by the inhabitants, especially by the women. The men and the boys wore drab clothes, with an occasional splash of colour – shirts and *dhotis;* tee-shirts with shorts or trousers. The small girls were sometimes in tee-

shirts too, but often wore long bright frocks. The grown women were a blaze of colour. Whether dressed in saris or *salwar-kameez*, they wore richly coloured fabrics. On closer inspection some of the cloth was threadbare or frayed, but nevertheless it looked very attractive in careful combinations of red and orange; yellow and green; pink and mauve. Even the widows looked good in their plain white saris.

The women did most of the work. The men had some jobs that were traditional, such as ploughing, but it was the women who weeded, harvested, gathered firewood, fed and milked the animals, carried water from the pump, and also did all the housework and looked after the children. Most of the women I saw were carrying a load on their heads – a basket of dung cakes; a brass or stainless steel water pot; a sheaf of millet – as well as carrying a pail or a child in a free hand. All were modest in demeanour, and at least half took care, when men might be around, to hide their faces behind their *ornis,* the headscarves of their saris.

The village was completely Hindu. There was a Brahman priest, and his family, who lived near the very small court-yarded brick temple. The rest of the villagers were Malahs, a low sub-caste who were traditionally fishermen and boatmen. Some still had boats. The men sometimes ate fish, but most of the time they had the vegetarian food – *chapatis* with spiced vegetables and pulses – that the women always cooked for themselves. No one seemed to eat meat. The main activity was small-scale farming. Moola's family had about three acres. As she was a widow, and Ramkali's husband was away, it was now being ploughed by cousins prior to sowing wheat. The house was even smaller than it had appeared when we first arrived. In total it could only have been twenty feet square, with two very small rooms and an internal courtyard. All the cooking was done on a tiny mud hearth, which was only large enough for a single pot. It seemed adequate, for I loved Ramkali's simple okra or aubergine dishes, served with wonderfully puffed *chapatis.*

Over the next week I visited many homes. I looked at crops and animals, went on the river, fished, visited the temple, looked at shrines, walked to neighbouring villages, and prac-tised my Hindi. I spent a good deal of time taking long walks across the fields. They were almost totally bare. An occasional neem tree, revered because of its medicinal properties, stood undisturbed; a solitary rock marked some ancient boundary. Otherwise nothing divided the smallholdings. Everywhere was cultivated. There were no hedges.

During that week, I met Moola's relatives and friends. At sunset we sat in front of the house, under the papaya trees, eating millet freshly roasted on the cob. I spoke to the elderly. I quizzed the Brahman. I met with the *sarpanches*, the men who had chaired the village council, and questioned them. None of them had ever heard of the Customs Hedge.

It was the time of Durga Puja. Durga, the earth goddess, was especially important in the village, for her blessing was needed to ensure the crops then being sown would flourish. Every evening there were musical gatherings, with *tabla*, cymbals, and harmonium, when hymns to her were sung.

21

Temporary shrines were full of supplicants. Inside, wooden arches enclosed colourful pictures of the goddess slaying Masishasur, the buffalo demon. On top of the arches seeds were sprouting. The temple was busy. Everyone was cheerful. It was a good time to meet people; to ask them if anyone in their family had ever spoken of the hedge. No one could help.

At first I was not too downcast. After all, I reasoned, the village was twenty miles from the line of the Customs Hedge. Communications were bad enough now – back in the nineteenth century people probably never stirred far from the village. Later, however, I began to think that the inhabitants would have needed salt, and since there seemed to be none locally, then someone must have brought it, and the news, in to the village. Surely the Customs Hedge, and the Salt Tax levied on crossing it, would have been something to report; something to bitterly complain about? It was puzzling.

I learnt that there was a Land Rover in Mangroy which was available for hire. In a four-wheel-drive vehicle, it might be possible to reach the line depicted on the India Office map, and then drive back and forth across that line to search for the remnants of the Customs Hedge. I booked it for a day.

On Friday, 18 October 1996, I set off to look for the hedge. We had been up since six. By seven, when the Land Rover was due, I had been for the customary walk to the land near the Yamuna for my ablutions, washed all over under the hand-pump, then breakfasted on *pakoras* and water-buffalo yoghurt. An hour later, there was still no sign of the vehicle. Santosh had to cycle to Mangrol to rouse the driver. He finally arrived at ten. Before we left, Moola sprinkled water on the sacred tulsi bush that grew on the veranda, and we said prayers. The Land Rover was full, for in addition to Santosh, the driver and me, there was the *sarpanch*, the driver's assistant, and two unknown hangers-on.

We drove west to Jalaun. From there I intended to follow the Customs Line, almost due north, to where it crossed the Yamuna, at Jagamapur. Just outside Jalaun we stopped on a crossroads, where we had tea at a stall. The road to our right went north to Surawun, Gohan, and Jagamapur. The line of the hedge should have been very close. The land was open, with large fields. There was no sign of any bushes or trees that might have been remnants of the hedge. The stall-owner knew nothing helpful.

We drove into town. The *sarpanch* knew an old shopkeeper who might be able to help. He was indeed old and knowl-edgeable, and he thought we might find the barrier we were looking for behind an ancient temple on the edge of the town. Finding a road to the temple was difficult. Eventually we made it there, only to find some old boundary stones in a quagmire. There was no sign at all of a hedge. To make sure, we traversed the land back and forth until we were back at the tea stall. We saw nothing.

We had more tea, and set off north. According to my copied map, we were very close to the line of the Customs Hedge. Occasionally, I saw what appeared to be a row of trees or bushes, but it turned out to be an illusion. At likely spots we abandoned the Land Rover and walked across the fields. There was nothing there.

Gohan was very small. Surely, I thought, the villagers would know something about the fort marked on the old map. We asked here and there, and eventually we did find some old men, smoking in a doorway, who remembered it. Yes, the English fort, they remembered it well – they gestured to a site just across the road – it had been demolished in the 1950s. A new house now occupied the spot. The men recollected the fort being used as a store, but had no idea as to its original function. We searched in vain for any signs of a hedge radiating out from the site.

At Jagamapur there was a derelict fort, probably Mughal, with views along the Yamuna. The land was sandy and uncultivated. Here, I felt, there was a better chance of finding the hedge intact. We drove slowly along the riverbank, upstream and then downstream, but all the trees and bushes stood seemingly at random.

My companions sought to cheer me up. We went into a Jagamapur restaurant. It was a hot day, and we drank delicious cold *lassi* made with full fat buttermilk and flavoured with rose water. Nevertheless, I remained depressed and

24

disappointed. It was nearly dusk. As we sped back, I peered into the fading landscape, hoping for a sudden lucky glimpse of the hedge, but it was not to be. It turned chilly. The wind rushed through the open-sided vehicle, and my companions wrapped themselves in their broad woollen shawls. Shivering, I berated myself for not being better prepared. At the village we had a major row with the driver, as to whether the hire charge included the cost of the diesel or not. We had to pay the extra. Although it was not a significant sum, the incident put me in an even worse mood.

I now knew, after my first search on the ground for the Customs Hedge, that what I really needed was a large-scale map. When I returned to England, I would search for one. Meanwhile, I decided to make one last effort – before returning to Delhi, I would go to Jhansi. The rough map I had with me showed the hedge – if, indeed, it was the line of the Customs Hedge – as going through Jhansi town. My guidebook referred to a fort dominating the town from 'a bare brown craggy hill'. Perhaps from there I might get an aerial view of the hedge, or see the line of its remnants.

It was, in any case, time for me to leave the village. I had been there ten days. Moola was to stay behind with her daughter. Santosh and I would go to Kalpi, then take the train south-west to Jhansi. I was sad to leave. It was a landmark in my Indian travels – I had been to a poor and truly remote Indian village, where no tourist had ever been. I had lived, for a short time, more or less like a villager. Far from merely surviving, I had enjoyed myself. My Hindi had also improved.

On one of the last days, I went for my early morning defeca-
tion. As I squatted, I looked out over the Yamuna and the sun
rose. I watched its redness reflected in the still water below.
Then, suddenly, I saw a huge crocodile. *'Magarmach!
Magarmach!'* I yelled, the Hindi coming without thinking. As
I hastily pulled up my trousers, farmers working nearby, and
then most of the village, ran to see the great beast. Such large
crocodiles were unusual. The remains of two partly cremated
bodies washed up on the riverbank had probably attracted it.
Corpses were often consigned to the rivers by families too
poor to pay for cremation firewood. I received a good deal of
praise for spotting the crocodile, and for my Hindi too. The
men chased it off in their fishing boats, until it was well down
the river.

I spent my last two days in the village going around to say
farewell to everyone. I told them that I would return, and I
meant it. On our last evening the Brahman priest invited us
for a meal. I was somewhat surprised since, of course, my
friends were low caste. His family served us with delicious
food, although they did not eat with us. It was a very
successful evening. The pretty teenage daughters gradually
lost their shyness, to reveal smiling faces from behind their
black shawls. Finally, they even posed for photographs. I
promised to send them copies from England.

On the day we left I rose at six. Moola took us to the
Bhairava shrine on the edge of the village to pray for a safe
journey, and that we might all meet again. She rubbed ochre
on to my forehead. I said my last *namastes* to Ramkali and her

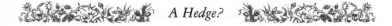

children – Mohan the grave small boy, and the irrepressible little Nanani, wide-eyed with excitement. Four of Santosh's friends had come with their bicycles to take us to Kalpi. It was a two-hour journey over rough paths and roads. Santosh and I rode side-saddle on two of the bicycles, while our baggage was strapped to the backs of the other two. From time to time we swapped around. Fortunately the Hero bicycles were incredibly strong, with double crossbars and frames. Fortunately, too, the weather had changed. It was no longer clear and hot, but overcast and cool. We rode singing and joking through flat country, dotted with tiny villages. Each village seemed to have a tea stall where they also repaired bikes. Everywhere the land was cultivated, open, and totally hedgeless.

We arrived in Kalpi in plenty of time for the ten-fifty train. I bought tickets for the ninety-mile journey to Jhansi. They were 29 rupees (50 pence) each. Then I took everyone for a gigantic breakfast. The young men consumed mountains of sticky sugar whorls, *jalebis*, to give them energy for the return journey. For me there was just time to look at an extraordinary complex of old memorials, with huge recumbent stone figures and walls topped with incredibly long undulating snakes. Their hoods, decorated with Lord Shiva's trident, guarded the gates.

Jhansi, despite its colourful history, was not particularly attractive. Most of the buildings were new and utilitarian. The Jhansi Hotel had probably been something in its heyday but was now in the middle of a crude refurbishment. Santosh, however, beamed with pleasure when he saw our room, for it had a large colour television, and he was avidly following the cricket. India was playing South Africa in a one-day match, and Santosh's hero, Tendulkar, looked set for a big score. The only building of note in the town seemed to be the fort, and that was lost in drizzling cloud. I cursed the change in the weather, which I had welcomed earlier. We postponed our visit to the fort until the following day, and watched India narrowly lose.

In the evening I telephoned Didi in Delhi, to discover that she had been taken ill and would be operated upon. It was not clear what was wrong. Her condition sounded serious, but not critical. I decided that whatever the visibility next day, we would leave Jhansi and return to Delhi. Leave, that was, if we could get seats on a train. It was necessary to make a reservation, and trains were often fully booked for several days ahead. I also needed to exchange money, which meant going to a bank.

The next morning was overcast, with low cloud obscuring the fort. However, it looked as though it would probably clear later. We breakfasted early, then went to the station booking office to catch it as it opened. In India, away from the major tourist towns, it could easily take all day to both secure a rail ticket and change money at a bank. We were pleasantly surprised to be given tickets within the hour. They were for

28

the afternoon train, at six o'clock. We even had time for a cup of tea before we hurried to the State Bank of India – the only bank that would cash travellers' cheques – to be there when it opened at ten.

We need not have rushed, for none of the employees turned up until ten-thirty, and it was eleven before we were let in. The service itself was prompter than usual. We were all finished at twelve-thirty, fortunately just before lunchtime, during which it would probably have been impossible to collect all the necessary counter-signatures needed for my minor transaction. We emerged from the bank to find that the cloud had partially lifted. The fort was in dappled sunshine. An auto-rickshaw took us up the hill, past a weird tableau of statues re-enacting the exploits of the Rani of Jhansi, to the great gate.

The seventeenth-century fort was huge. The British had reinforced the already massive stone ramparts with enormous gun-emplacements. Other nineteenth- and twentieth-century British additions filled the inside, nestling alongside the original palace and temple. I felt sorry for the British soldiers garrisoning the dubiously acquired fortress, who had been confined in that massive suntrap. I saw a cluster of tourists around a notice on top of one of the ramparts, and went over to look. It was above a forty-foot drop on to steeply sloped earth. It was written in Hindi, and in English: 'Rani Jhansi jumped from this place on the horse back with her adopted son.'

The Rani of Jhansi had been widowed in 1853. The British – then always looking for ways to expand – had enacted a law by which Jhansi lapsed to them because she had no natural son. This was despite her having, as had often been done by rulers before, adopted a son. She was pensioned off, but came back in the 'Mutiny' to reclaim her heritage. Leading 500 warriors, she captured the fortress. Thousands of British soldiers were killed. Eventually the British managed to reclaim the fort. The rani escaped on horseback and 'dressed like a man . . . holding her sword two-handed and holding the reins of her horse in her teeth' died in battle at Gwalior.

The visibility from the ramparts was far from perfect. From time to time, however, as the low cloud shifted, it offered a view for several miles. There were numerous individual and clumped trees. Try as I did, looking first to the north and then to the south, I was unable to make any kind of line out of them. Then the cloud descended again. It began to drizzle. Depressed, we went back to the hotel to pack. Travelling once again by Shatabdi Express, we were back in Delhi by ten-thirty that evening.

I spent much of the next week visiting Didi in hospital. By the end of it she was almost recovered. She listened cheerfully to all our adventures, while Santosh and I ate the meals she was unable to consume. We drank countless cups of tea as we

made plans for me to come back the following year to continue the search. However, I knew that, before I returned, I must definitely find that large-scale and detailed map of the Customs Hedge. Otherwise, I would be wasting my time.

On the plane back to London, I had lots of time to think about the hedge. At first, my efforts to find it had been driven by not much more than coincidence. Although I had been fascinated by its bizarre history, it was the proximity to the village that I had already arranged to visit that had spurred me on. Now that I had failed to find any sign of it near there, I might have dropped the whole project. But no, for some inexplicable reason, the setback had only made me more determined. I had already decided to return to India in 1997 to hunt for the hedge. I knew that better maps were needed, and I intended to search hard for them. I would not be able to take any leave until towards the end of the year, so there would be plenty of time. I also intended to delve into the broader history. How had people's lives been affected by the Customs Hedge and the Salt Tax?

The Salt Tax

A monopoly of the necessaries of life, in any hands whatever, more especially in the hands of the English, who are possessed of such an overruling influence, is liable to the greatest abuses.

DIRECTORS OF THE EAST INDIA COMPANY TO LORD CLIVE

The Salt Tax was born out of British greed: first, out of the individual greed of the servants of the East India Company; later, out of the greed of the Company itself, and its shareholders; finally, out of the greed of the British government, its parliament, and its electors. The Honourable East India Company was founded as a commercial enterprise in 1600 under a royal charter from Queen Elizabeth I. Various seventeenth-century charters gave the Company extraordinary privileges to further trade in the east. It had the power to mint money, and had legal jurisdiction over its employees. Most importantly, it could raise its own army and navy, and could make war or peace with non-Christian states. In its early years, however, it used these powers sparingly, and was reluc-

33

tant to stray into costly non-commercial ventures. It confined its activities to fighting European rivals, and to the establishment of trading posts on the Indian coast. It was not until the middle of the eighteenth century that the Company began to have the major territorial ambitions that eventually resulted in it assuming the government of India, and imposing taxes on its people.

During the nineteenth century, the East India Company acquired more and more territory to administer. As it did so, however, the British parliament and government exercised more and more control over the Company. In 1835, the Company's charter came up for renewal. After that, the Company virtually became an agent of the British government, administering India and collecting taxes on its behalf. This anomalous position came to an end with the 'Indian Mutiny' of 1857, and the British government took over direct control of the Company's territories the following year. Throughout these changes, the tax system established by the Company continued largely unaltered, with the two principal taxes being those levied on land and on salt.

Salt had been taxed in India from time immemorial. The Maurya king, Chandragupta, who ruled much of India from 324 to 301 BC, imposed taxes on salt. The *Arthasastra,* a treatise on governance, which is believed to have been largely composed by his chief minister, Kautilya, lists all the duties of the state's officials. It goes into incredible detail: it specifies the times of day that state elephants are to be bathed; it advises what type of widows should be recruited as spies. A special officer, the *lavanadhyaksa,* was responsible for salt. Licences for manufacture were issued, for a fee, or in exchange for one-sixth of the output. In addition, like on many other products, a tax was levied by the difference between 'the King's measure' and 'the common measure'. This imposed an extra 5 per cent tax. Taxes were also imposed on imported salt so that there was no loss to the treasury. It seems, therefore, that the tax on salt was about 25 per cent in total. Taxes of this magnitude, or less, seem to have been imposed over most of India until the arrival of the British.

In Bengal there had been a small tax on salt under the Mughals – 5 per cent for Hindus, 2½ per cent for Muslims – levied as it passed up the River Ganges to the interior. In addition, some inland rulers levied a small toll on salt, and other goods, as they entered their territory. All these taxes, however, were only sporadically and inefficiently collected. The overall tax burden on salt was minor, and not a hardship. With the British it was to be different.

In 1756 the Nawab of Bengal had driven the Company out of its trading post at Calcutta. The following year, Robert Clive led the Company's army to victory over the nawab at Plassey, a hundred miles north of Calcutta. This enabled the Company to re-establish itself in Calcutta. In 1759 the Company acquired land nearby on which there were salt works. As a form of tax, the company doubled the ground rent, and also imposed a small transit duty. Eventually this was consolidated, with other impositions, to give a total tax of less than one-fifth of a rupee per *maund*, an ancient measure of about 82 imperial pounds weight.

Very little of the tax was collected, however, for the Company's European employees and other British merchants were, by the treaty forced on the Mughals, exempt from this and other taxes. They traded on their own account on a vast scale in dutiable goods, claiming exemption from all taxes and transit duties. Naturally, this enabled them to corner much of the trade. They were able to sell at a discount and undercut Indian businessmen. Even though they did eventually have to pay 2½ per cent to the local government, they were able to accumulate massive personal fortunes. In addition to trading on their own account, they also sold rights in duty-free trade to sub-agents. They, and their sub-agents, set up duty-free trading posts, known as 'factories'. Worst of all, they used private armies to force peasants and merchants – who, in any case, were no longer allowed to sell to foreigners – to sell cheaply. As the nawab, Mir Kasim, wrote:

In every pargana, every village and every factory, they buy and sell salt, betel nut, ghee, rice, straw, bamboo, fish, gunnies, ginger, sugar, tobacco, opium, and many other things. They forcibly take away the goods and commodities of the ryots and merchants for a fourth part of their value . . . they oblige the ryots to give five rupees for goods which are worth but one rupee . . . near four or five hundred new factories have been established . . . they expose my government to scorn and are the greatest detriment to me.

All this was done by the Company's servants, not to enrich the Company, but to enrich themselves. In their defence it must be said that salaries of 50 or 100 rupees a year were hardly sufficient, and the Company expected them to be augmented. The scale of the supplementation was, however, totally excessive. The example was set by Robert Clive himself.

When Clive defeated the nawab, he had then put a puppet, Mir Jafar, one of the nobles, on the throne. In return, Clive had received from the traitor 2,340,000 rupees, rentals of 300,000 rupees a year, and an 880-square-mile private estate. This was all given to Clive personally. Thirty-two years old, he instantly became one of the richest of all Englishmen. He then took steps to stop the Company from ever appropriating his spoils. In 1760 he went back to England and bought control of the Company. At the same time he also purchased enough rotten boroughs – seats where the small number of electors made it possible to easily bribe a majority – so that he, and his Company, became almost immune from parliamentary control.

While Clive was consolidating his position in London – in 1762 he became Lord Clive of Plassey – the people of India continued to be bled. Mir Jafar, appalled at what was happening to the country, abdicated. Mir Kasim replaced him. In return for the Company's support, he agreed to pay the Company 5,000,000 rupees a year in silver. This had to be raised by taxing the people. Meanwhile, the Company's employees looted and pillaged the country with more and more ferocity. By 1762 even Mir Kasim was appalled. He attacked the Company merchants. The other Mughal princes, seeing what might happen to them, joined him. The Company's army raced to defend its own. In 1764 the armies met between Varanasi and Patna, at Baksar. The combined forces of the Mughals were totally defeated. It was the end of the Mughals as the dominant power, and the beginning of British rule.

The Company allowed the Mughal emperor in Delhi to continue as nominal ruler, but took away his income. The Company took over the administration – the *Diwani* – and became the feudal lord. It was to receive the land revenue, which was the principal tax, and the other minor taxes. All the revenues of greater Bengal – which included Bihar and Orissa – were to go into the Company's coffers. It inherited the rights to an income of tens of millions of rupees. Its own employees, however, were expropriating much of that income.

Clive returned to India in 1765. He found that the country had been rendered almost ungovernable by the depredations in his absence: 'such a scene of anarchy, confusion, bribery, corruption, and extortion was never seen or heard of in any country but Bengal; nor such and so many fortunes acquired in so unjust and rapacious a manner.' Here, indeed, was the pot calling the kettle black! Clive banned bribes and lavish gifts. The right to claim exemption from taxes and duties was severely curtailed. It was restricted to the Company's European staff, and only to those with more than five years' service.

Old habits, however, died hard. Clive knew that, if he was to clean up the administration and also keep his colleagues happy, he must find money to augment meagre salaries. He was also not averse to making more money for himself and his friends. In 1765 he established the 'Exclusive Company'. This was a private company whose profits would be shared among the Company's senior servants – sixty-one civil administrators, military men, doctors, and clergy – in proportion to their seniority. There were fifty-six one-third shares. The Governor, Clive himself, was to have the largest allocation, of five shares. The most junior eligible servants would receive one-third of a share. The new company was given a total monopoly to make what profit it could, on tobacco, betel nut, and salt. For the first time salt, an essential item of diet, was to be significantly taxed. The poor, as well as the rich, would be affected. All production of salt, and of betel nut and tobacco, other than for the Exclusive Company, was prohibited. Contracts were given to deliver salt to depots. Merchants then had to buy all their requirements from these depots, before selling them on to where they could best make a profit.

All this was in defiance of instructions from London: 'We consider it as too disgraceful, and below the dignity of the present situation, to allow of such a monopoly.' It took, however, about six months for a ship to reach London, and often longer, and another six months to return with instructions. Clive tried to buy off opposition by giving the Company 1,200,000 rupees per annum of the profits.

London, however, was implacable: 'a monopoly of the necessaries of life, in any hands whatever, more especially in the hands of the English, who are possessed of such an overruling influence, is liable to the greatest abuse.' On 1

September 1767 the Exclusive Society relinquished its monopoly on tobacco and betel nut. On 7 October 1768 it finally gave up its monopoly on salt. In the years of its operation it made the huge profit of 6,731,170 rupees.

The Exclusive Company had used its monopoly to raise the wholesale price of salt at its depots from 1.25 rupees to 2.47 rupees a *maund* of 82 pounds. When the monopoly was abolished the price fell again to 1.48 rupees. The duty payable to the East India Company was also reduced, from 50 per cent to 0.3 rupees a *maund*. The East India Company's revenue fell dramatically. As an official investigation revealed:

> A large part (if not the whole) of this decrease of revenue must be attributed to the malaversions of the 'Exclusive Company' which long after its authority to manufacture had ceased, on the pretext of selling off its old stock of salt, interfered with the business of the honest trader, and which, in six years from its constitution in 1765, smuggled salt to such an extent as to defraud the Government of duty to an aggregate amount estimated by the Committee of Secrecy in 1773 at upwards of 40 lakhs of rupees.

Clive left for England in 1767. His riches attracted great adverse comment. By the standards of the English landowners, his wealth was not extraordinary, but he had accumulated it too fast. Some people, indeed, believed that he had made a pact with the devil. A commission of enquiry into

his conduct in India was set up. It ended with the House of Commons voting that he 'had rendered great and praiseworthy services to his country'. He developed stomach pains and took large doses of opium. In 1774, at the age of forty-nine, Clive cut his own throat with a penknife. He was buried in an unmarked grave.

It was true that Clive was partly brought down by the envy of rich Englishmen, who themselves had bled their own pitifully poor tenants for generations. It must, however, also be remembered that Clive's wealth had come indirectly from the Indian peasants, who earned a fraction of what was earned by their English counterparts. An agricultural labourer in England earned perhaps the equivalent of 15 rupees (£1.50) a month, whereas the Indian labourer received only 1 rupee. What was more, the money was taken out of the country. That was to become the norm. Richard Barwell, one of Clive's colleagues, who made 400,000 rupees a year from illicit salt contracts, brought an estimated 6,000,000 rupees back to England. British individuals, and most of all the East India Company itself, took vast sums out of India and spent it in Britain. Jobs that might have been created in India, had the money been spent there, were given to workmen in Britain. India, which when the British arrived had been relatively well off, became much poorer.

41

In 1770 famine hit Bengal. The land revenue had only been sporadically collected by the Mughals, especially in times of difficulty. After the Company took over the *Diwani* it was fully and ruthlessly collected. In 1769 the crop was poor. In 1770, after six months without rain, the crop almost totally failed. There has never been a failure of crops all over India. Local shortages can always be rectified if there is money to buy in grain. However, following the looting of Bengal by the Company and its employees, money was extremely scarce. The Company had no mercy; it took its dues in full. As people began to die, the amount of land revenue due from the survivors increased. It was so fiercely collected that many had to sell their seed corn. Out of the millions they collected, the Company gave back 90,000 rupees in famine relief – 90,000 rupees for 30,000,000 people.

Meanwhile, the Company's employees and their agents cornered the rice market. They bought up rice in those areas where the crop had not failed, warehoused it under armed guard, and sold to those with the most money. The price of a *maund* (82 pounds) of rice rose from about 0.4 to 13 rupees. The wealthier Indians exchanged their savings and jewellery for food. The peasants and labourers, who only earned 1 or, at the most, 2 rupees a month, perished. Between one-third and one-half of the entire population – at least ten million people – died. The Salt Tax was, of course, still collected by the Company in full on the salt that was consumed. However, many could not afford to buy salt. In any case, the supply of salt was severely disrupted by the death of so many salt workers, bullock cart drivers, and boatmen.

After the famine, the country took many years to recover. Many Indians, although alive, had come close to death and remained ill. Children were stunted. The Company, however, was determined to allow no relaxation in the collection of the land revenue. The landlords had to extort the money from a severely depleted population. In many cases they found it impossible, and abandoned the land to revert to jungle. Crops were forbidden to be planted if the tax had not been paid. Large numbers of desperate people took to banditry. From being one of the most law-abiding populations, Bengal and its hinterland became full of robbers and smugglers. These smugglers were eventually to become a major problem for the British when they sought to increase the revenue from salt.

The free, but taxed, manufacture and trade in salt continued until 1772. From 1767, when Clive left, to 1772, the Company had been administered by men of little ability. The country was largely ungoverned. More importantly, from the British government's perspective, the Company had been unable to pay its taxes in England. More money had to be extracted from India. In 1772 Warren Hastings was appointed to control the Company's affairs in Bengal. The following year, as the head of a new Council, he also took charge of the Company's interests in the Bombay and Madras Presidencies, and was given the title of Governor-General.

Hastings had joined the Company in 1750. He was fluent in several Indian languages, and was brilliant, ambitious and ruthless. He realised that his position was dependent on the Company in London receiving more money. He also recognised the threat to the Company's interests from the Maratha rulers in the west, who were being aided by the French. To fight wars, and guarantee the Company's position, he needed money. His priority, therefore, was to consolidate and expand the Company's revenues. His first acts were to cut in half the stipend of the powerless nawab and to stop altogether the annual tribute Clive had promised to the emperor in Delhi. He changed the whole system of revenue collection, so that the land revenue and other taxes were collected directly by the Company. These changes made the Company 5,000,000 rupees a year better off. When Hastings took control, in 1772, salt was still being freely manufactured, and taxed at 0.3 rupees a *maund*. The revenue was only 450,000 rupees a year. Hastings determined to raise it.

The Company once again took over control of the manufacture of salt. The salt works, however, were leased out to 'farmers', who under various complicated arrangements agreed to deliver salt at a fixed price to the Company. The Company sold the leases to the highest bidders. Corrupt practices of the Company's staff, and collusion between bidders, ensured the failure of the system. By 1780 salt revenue had fallen to 80,000 rupees. Moreover the salt worker, the *malangis*, had been cruelly exploited. Sixty thousand men, often coming from families that had been independent salt-makers for generations, had suddenly found their businesses expropriated, and been forced to work for pitiful wages. News of their plight even caused outrage in England.

In 1780 Hastings bought the whole process of salt manu-

44

facture and taxation under direct government control. He devised a system that, fundamentally unaltered, was to last until the British left. The salt-producing areas were put under a Comptroller and divided into Agencies. Each Agency was placed under the control of an Agent, a government officer. They were salaried, but also received a commission of ten per cent on the profit obtained by the government. The *malangis*, now self-employed again, delivered the salt to the Agents at an agreed price. The Agents then sold the salt on to wholesalers at a price decided by the government. This price was fixed at 2 rupees a *maund*. As the *malangis* received from 0.5 to 0.9 rupees for their salt, the 'tax' was 1.1 to 1.5 rupees a *maund*. From the Company's point of view, the new method was a complete success. In its first year, 1781–2, the salt revenue was 2,960,130 rupees. By 1784–5 the revenue had risen to the huge amount of 6,257,470 rupees.

The Company became dependent on its income from salt. When Lord Cornwallis took over as Governor-General, he saw another way to increase income. It had become the habit of the wholesalers to take advantage of their sub-monopoly and force up the price of salt. In 1788, instead of fixing the price in advance, the Company took to selling to the wholesalers by auction. This had the effect of hugely increasing the tax to 3.25 rupees a *maund*. It remained around this extraordinary level until 1879. In thirty years, therefore, the Company had forced up a sporadically collected minor tax into one that was ruthlessly collected at a punitive rate. The wholesale price of salt increased from 1.25 rupees to about 4 rupees a *maund*. To this wholesale price, of course, the profit of the retailer and the cost of transport had to be added. All this occurred at a time when famine and unemployment swept Bengal; when hugely increased land rents were extorted by the Company; and when an agricultural labourer's wages were, if he were employed, 1 or 2 rupees a month.

The amount of salt used by an Indian family was the subject of fierce argument. The Company, seeking to minimise opposition to taxing such a necessity, tried to show that 12 pounds a head per year was adequate. Others argued that 16 pounds was a more realistic figure. Certainly, when price was not a consideration, consumption rose above that figure. There was argument as to whether Indian cattle or sheep needed salt. The size of an average family was another point of contention. However, at the lower end of the scale, it is reasonable to assume that a small family, of two adults and three children, needed at least half a *maund* of salt, 41 pounds a year. Half a *maund* of salt, in 1788, retailed for 2 rupees or more – two months' income for many families. This situation continued for many years, and agrees with the evidence given to a Parliamentary Select Committee of 1836 by Dr John Crawfurd of the Bengal Medical Service: 'I estimate that the cost of salt to the rural labourer, i.e. to the great mass of the people of Bengal, for a family, as being equal to about two months' wages, i.e. $\frac{1}{6}$ of the whole annual earnings.' Many other families, following the disasters that had beset the country, were totally without money. In some years the situation was even worse, for until 1836 when the auction system was changed, sub-monopolies caused periodic escalations in price. 'In 1823, for example,' Crawfurd records, 'in many parts of the country the price rose to 12 rupees a *maund* for adulterated salt.' At that price, half a *maund* of salt would have cost half a year's wages!

At the end of the eighteenth century British power in India was exercised from three main centres – Bengal, Madras, and Bombay. Originally they were independent of each other but, under Warren Hastings, brought more together. Nevertheless, they continued to have an extraordinary degree of financial autonomy. The Bengal government severely limited its options to raise money when it created the Permanent Settlement of 1793. That legislation permanently fixed the land tax of the hereditary overlords, the *zamindars*. As land values increased with inflation and development, the government's revenues stagnated. Consequently, Bengal had to find other sources of taxation. It chose salt. The other presidencies were able gradually to raise the land tax and avoid a swingeing Salt Tax. Generally, until the Salt Tax was equalised in 1879, their levy was less than a third of that in greater Bengal. The Salt Tax in the Bengal Presidency remained at a punitively high level for ninety years.

As the Company enforced its monopoly and raised the price

of salt, others tried to supply it more cheaply. There were three main ways to obtain salt illegally. It could be stolen, and certainly some was filched from government and other warehouses. It could be surreptitiously manufactured, either at the regular salt works, or elsewhere. With its long shoreline, Bengal gave plenty of scope. Or it could be smuggled in from outside the Company's domains. This last option was to prove the greatest threat to the Company's revenues. The inhabitants of greater Bengal were desperate for affordable salt. The Company was determined to raise the maximum revenue and block off any illicit supply. The stage was set for an epic battle, which would lead to the creation of the Customs Hedge.

Maps

*And my father now and then sending me small sums of
money, I laid them out in learning navigation and other
parts of the mathematics useful to those who intend to
travel.*

JONATHAN SWIFT, *Gulliver's Travels*

B ack in London I searched for maps of the hedge. The
librarians I consulted were not even aware of the existence of the Customs Hedge, so I had to start from scratch. I
combed the printed and annotated map catalogue of the India
Office Library assiduously, week after week, from beginning
to end. I requested any item even remotely relevant, since
descriptions were often misleading. The long-suffering but
remarkably courteous staff brought up countless unwieldy
portfolios for my perusal. All my effort produced almost
nothing that was useful. Occasionally, I found a line on a map
produced before 1879 which might, or might not, have been
the Customs Line. Invariably the scale was too small to be
helpful. The highly detailed sheets of *The Indian Atlas* showed

nothing, even though some were only dated slightly later than 1879, the year the hedge was abandoned. I found it diffi-cult to believe that nothing was left, even then.

The one map of interest I found was an 1870 'Map of Jaloun District'. This was extremely unusual since the names on it were in both Urdu and Hindi scripts. Although coloured in very prettily, it was not detailed enough to be of much use in the field. However, it seemed to show the Customs Hedge, which followed much the same path that I had already trav-elled. I could not read Urdu, but the Devanagari script of the Hindi for the Customs Line transliterated to *parmat lain.* I looked *parmat* up in *The Oxford Hindi–English Dictionary,* where the entry read: *'parmat* (Engl. *Permit*), m. f. 1. Permit. 2. *Pl* customs post.' I made a note of the term, for use in India.

I also searched the many gazetteers. The District Gazetteers of India were a mine of information. At various dates volumes of several hundred pages were produced by the British on each of the many hundreds of administrative districts of India. Those for 1909, produced at the zenith of Imperial rule, are perhaps the most comprehensive, and occupy bays of shelving. Each volume has chapters on the history, agricul-ture, industry, culture and finances of the district, plus a section on each town and notes on major villages. They go into incredible detail, and incorporate a census of occupation, caste and religion. There are often photographs and maps. Earlier gazetteers, out of which these grew, were generally briefer, but still contained a wealth of detail. The Customs Line went through dozens of districts as it wound its way across India, so there was a vast mass of information to trawl. I did come across some references, such as 'the Imperial Customs Line formerly passed close by . . .', but nothing specific enough to be of real help. I searched in vain for useful maps or photographs.

I combed the various name indexes to see if there were any archives of personal papers from any of the customs officers listed in the Annual Reports or *The India List*, but there I also drew a blank. By accident, I came across a record of a Private George Moxham – the same name as my father – who had served in Her Majesty's Thirty-first Foot Regiment, and was buried near Varanasi, 'at Ghazeepore'. I assumed he must be a relative, and thought it might be interesting to try and find his grave one day. But that would have to wait.

Feeling that I had, for the time being at least, exhausted the resources of the India Office Library, I turned my attention to the main collections of the British Library. The computerised catalogue enabled me to search for books using various key words. I searched painstakingly for books under various combinations of 'India', 'salt', 'tax', 'customs', and so forth. I had to filter through thousands of book titles. The search word 'customs' was particularly troublesome, because of its alternative meanings. I had to sort through and discard hundreds of books on sociology and religion.

I found many interesting accounts of travels in nineteenth-century India, but nothing to help in my search for the precise location of the hedge. I had a moment of excitement when I came across a book *Past Days in India*, described as being 'By a late Customs' Officer, N.W. Provinces, India'. Full of expectation, I ordered it. It turned out to be a book of reminiscences solely devoted to hunting. It gave me some amusement, as the author emphasised the horrendous prospects facing a poorly supervised expedition, where one might find oneself without sufficient wine or brandy. There was not, however, even a passing reference to the Customs Department, or to the Customs Line.

At the India Office Library, the Annual Reports of the Inland Customs Department, which had been so useful, seemed to be incomplete. The last volume they had was for the official year 1877–8. The Customs Line had been abandoned a year later, in April 1879. I was keen to find the volume covering that last year, since it might have important information about the demise of the Customs Hedge. Perhaps some of it had been destroyed to make a road; perhaps some had been cut and sold off for firewood. Just before I left Delhi, I had searched the Indian National Archive for the missing volume, but without success. Back in London I searched catalogues of libraries in London, and beyond, but again was unsuccessful. Perhaps it had never been compiled or printed.

I continued my searches for the precise location of the Customs Line throughout the early part of 1997, but without success. My friends and colleagues pulled my leg about my obsessive research. Some of them were sympathetic, but others obviously thought the hedge was a figment of my imagination. One particular colleague took to

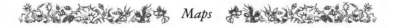

mocking me as I walked past his desk: 'A thousand-mile hedge across India? That's right, Roy. You keep on looking!' The gloom of the winter months took its toll on me. Even when things were going well, my mood tended to be adversely affected by low light levels. My lack of success in my researches further depressed me. It was spring before the situation improved.

On the first day of April, I visited the Royal Geographical Society in Kensington Gore. I had always assumed it was a private library for members only, and that it would be difficult to gain access to the map collection, but they were most welcoming. The librarian, however, was doubtful if they would have anything that was not already at the India Office Library. Fortunately he was mistaken. I found three hopeful entries in an old ledger. They were all, for the early date, maps of a much larger scale than I had previously seen. The ones of Saugor District in 1870, and of Hoshangabad District in 1871, although very detailed, failed to show the Customs Line. I felt very dispirited as I waited for the last of my requests – a map of Agra District.

It was a massive map – nine sheets, each three feet by two. It had to be laid out on a large table in the hallway. The table was in front of a massive marble fireplace surmounted, appropriately enough, by an oil painting of Lord Curzon just before he became Viceroy of India. The sheets were dated April 1879, the very month the Customs Line was abandoned. That was perfect for me since, if it showed the often-changed line, it would show it in its final form. The scale was one inch to the mile, and there was extraordinary detail. In Agra town, for example, the layout of the gardens around the Taj Mahal was clearly visible.

I soon saw what I was looking for. Across three sheets of the map there was a double line, as if for a road, with a line of tree-like symbols above it. To my delight, it was clearly labelled – 'Old Custom's Line'. It was wonderful to see those words. Coming from the north-west, the line followed the Yamuna River, keeping several miles south. It ran close to Mathura, then a few miles south of Agra, and on to Fatehabad, before it crossed the River Utangan, to go off the edge of the map, heading south-east. Altogether on the three sheets there were fifty miles of the Customs Hedge. At last!

Roads, railways, and canals were also clearly shown, as were the smallest villages. It seemed to me, there in the hallway of the Royal Geographical Society, with the maps spread out across the great polished wood table, that I had at last found what I needed. Surely, I thought, I could not fail to find the Customs Hedge with a map like that. What was more, the maps were edged with scales of latitude and longitude. The scales were graduated into minutes of a degree. Each minute – representing about a mile – was at least an inch long, and easily sub-dividable. I envisaged being able to fix the latitude and longitude of any point on the Customs Line to within a hundred yards. On the ground, it should be easy to find.

Suddenly, I had a nasty thought. How was I going to copy the map? To take advantage of its detail I needed a good repro-duction. My experiences at the India Office had warned me that permission to make a photocopy might not be forthcoming. As a conservator, myself, I was only too aware of the dangers of photocopying old and rare documents. At work, I had often found myself refusing permission to copy material. It was a change to be on the other side of the fence. Fortunately, the map was in excellent condition. However, the size of the sheets might present a problem, for they were too large for most photocopiers. Would a photograph be a possibility? But, then, would I lose the proper scale? Would the staff, perhaps, allow me to make a tracing? Perhaps they did not allow any copying at all. It was, of course, All Fools' Day, and fate might have shown me the maps, only then to make them unavailable.

With some trepidation, I went to consult the man who had issued the map.

'Umm . . . err . . . I was wondering . . . would it be, err, perhaps, be possible to copy these?'

'Oh, yes,' he said brightly. 'We've an extra-large photocopier. I'll do them straight away. How many do you want?'

A few minutes later I was strolling across Kensington Gardens with a large bundle of reproduced maps under my arm. It was a perfect spring day and warm in the sun.

Now I had the map I had so desperately desired, I needed to learn how to read it. Seeing the Customs Hedge on the map was all very well, but I had to be sure that I would be able to find my way there. At first sight it looked easy enough. Like any map, it resembled a simplified aerial photograph. However, it was soon apparent that there would be nowhere I could stand to look down on the terrain. The land around the hedge was extremely flat. Although the map had no contours, there were numerous spots with the height recorded against them. They were all about 550 feet above sea level, and varied by only 20 feet. Hills would have been easy to locate, and would have given a panoramic view of the countryside. There were none.

At the time the map was drawn, it would have been relatively easy to navigate from it. However, over a hundred years later, much would have changed. Roads, railways and canals would have been built, demolished, or realigned. The only constant landmarks would be the villages and towns. I decided, therefore, that my best bet would be to go to various villages near the Customs Line, and then walk across country. The land was so flat, so featureless, that to go in the right direction I would need a compass.

I had never used a map and compass before, so I needed a good manual. I looked in various bookshops, but found the volumes on hill walking and mountaineering inadequate or difficult to understand. It was in the university library that I found the perfect book – the War Office *Manual of Map Reading.* This small thin volume had everything I needed to know. Rather unfairly, the authors were not credited, for it was a model of layout and simple prose. Impressed by the War Office's expertise, I bypassed the flashy, fragile, and expensive new compasses on offer, and bought a second-hand army prismatic compass.

I did not, however, completely shun new technology. A yachtsman friend spoke enthusiastically of Global Positioning System (GPS) navigators. These use a constellation of satellites to obtain a longitude and latitude fix anywhere in the world. Providing there is a clear view of the sky, they are extremely accurate. You could get a position accurate to within a hundred yards. They would have been more accurate, except that the United States government, which owned the system, had built in random inaccuracies to limit non-authorised military use. Even so, during the Gulf War they had turned off the system.

The price of a basic GPS navigator had recently come down to £125. So, trusting that another war was not looming, I bought one. It was a fine piece of modern engineering, fitting snugly into the palm of the hand. You pressed the button and, a minute later, the longitude and latitude came up on the little screen. It had many other features. From my point of view, the most important was that I could key in a longitude and latitude, and then the machine would give the direction and distance to it. I intended to take co-ordinates of the Customs Hedge off the 1879 map, and then use the GPS navigator to walk to them. First, however, I needed some practice.

The War Office book and the GPS manual made it all seem easy. In practice it was not so simple. I had to spend many weekends wandering across fields to get proficient. I learnt to

take bearings with the compass; to find landmarks on an
Ordnance Survey map with the GPS navigator. I practised on
flat terrain, where it was difficult to spot things from afar by
eye. With more and more confidence I was able to navigate
my way to a statue in Hyde Park; to an isolated ruin near to
my mother's house in the Vale of Evesham.

Armed with a decent map, and reasonably confident of my
skills in map-reading, I arranged to go to India that
November. It should be relatively cool and dry. In my
remaining spare time, I made frequent visits to libraries to try
and unearth more information. Once again I was struck by
how little had been written about the Customs Hedge.
Highly detailed books on the difficulties of trading across
nineteenth-century India hardly mentioned it; monumental
histories of the salt industry in India merely gave it a few
lines. The multi-volumed histories of India, issued by the
universities of Oxford and Cambridge, virtually ignored it.

Late in October, on my last weekend in England, I made a
discovery in the India Office Library. I found a gazetteer that
had previously escaped my attention. That was because,
instead of being described as a gazetteer, it had the grand title
*North-Western Provinces – a statistical, descriptive and historical
account.* It was in fourteen thick volumes, each bearing a
different date from 1874 to 1886. There was a map for each of
the dozens of administrative districts, each one stretching
across a double page. The maps in the later volumes, after the
demise of the Customs Line, were of no help. Even if traces of
the Customs Line had remained, they were not shown. The

earlier volumes were more helpful. I found four maps with a stripe running across, clearly lettered 'Customs Line'. They were of Jalaun District, 1874; Jhansi District, 1874; Lalatpur [Lalitpur] District, 1874; and Etawa [Etawah] District, 1876. Unfortunately, they were not very detailed, and only of a scale of eight miles to the inch.

The Jalaun map showed me nothing new. It confirmed the information on the maps that I had used for my previous trip. There was slightly more detail, but not enough to justify my revisiting the district. The other maps were more interesting, adding a lot to my knowledge of the whereabouts of the Customs Line. Unfortunately, the volumes were all very tightly bound. It was impossible to see right into the gutters of the books. What could be seen, could not easily be photo-copied. It might have been possible to take some kind of photograph, but there was no time to arrange that before I departed. I was leaving the next week. I searched the various computer catalogues of the libraries in the university. At the very last moment, I found the Jhansi volume in the library of the Institute of Commonwealth Studies. The Archivist was most helpful, and brought it over to me at the main University Library. There we had just purchased a digital photocopier which safely produced an excellent copy. I was happy with just that one map as a fallback, for I was already confident that the much larger-scale map of Agra District would lead me to the remains of the Customs Hedge.

I spent many hours keying in the precise longitude and latitude co-ordinates of the Customs Hedge into the GPS navigator. The more I studied the Agra map through a magnifying glass, and the more I looked at the little drawings of trees that delineated the Customs Line, the more certain I became that it would lead me to the hedge.

FOUR

The Customs Line

*There grew up gradually a monstrous system to which it
would be almost impossible to find a parallel in any toler-
ably civilised country.*

JOHN AND RICHARD STRACHEY,
The Finances and Public Works of India

T here were several decades of action against the salt smugglers before the idea of establishing a Customs Hedge
emerged. In order to check the smuggling of salt, and collect
the customs duty on sugar, tobacco and other minor items,
the East India Company set up customs houses throughout
greater Bengal. A law of 1803 provided for the establishment
of a customs house, or *chowkey*, in every administrative
district. The following year, a new law stipulated that 'The
Collectors of the Government customs shall establish custom-
house *chowkies* at such places as may be deemed necessary on
the principal routes or ghauts leading to or from their respec-
tive customs-houses.' Customs barriers were then erected on
every major road and river in the Bengal Presidency.

These *rowannah chowkies* (named for the *rowannahs,* or passes, they issued to certify duty had been paid), were supplemented by preventative *chowkies.* These were erected near to legal salt works to prevent salt being smuggled out. They were also put into areas near the sea, and on salt-rich earth, where salt might be illegally manufactured.

The officers in charge of the customs houses were given every incentive to be vigilant. The law provided that they should 'be entitled to a reward of thirty-five per cent on the value of salt which shall be attached and confiscated'. Under proper control the Customs Department might have functioned efficiently. In line with usual practice, however, the Company failed to give an adequate salary to the junior staff. The Company must have realised that this would lead to abuses, and it did. An English observer wrote:

There never was a service in a state of such utter degradation as the subordinate native officers in the customs department. They may be said to have no salary at all, for what remains of the miserable pittance, after deducting the expense of paper, pens and ink, is swallowed up by the premium paid to cover the risk of their surety, and this the obligation of the furnished security, which is intended to form an additional safeguard against malaversion, only imposes upon them a stronger necessity to have recourse to corrupt practices for their sustenance. Bands of customs-house officers were therefore let loose, without any regular allowances, upon the trade and communications of the country, to derive the best subsistence they can from extortion and collusion . .

Owing nothing to the Government, they do not consider themselves under any obligation to keep faith with it. When a person has once entered the line, all regard for character is dismissed, and he considers only how much he can make of his time, for as also is the case with hangmen and other persons following disreputable professions, the loss of character must be made up by ample pecuniary gains.

The officers had wide powers of search and arrest, which they used to extort bribes. The senior well-paid officers tried to exercise some control, but as soon as they turned their backs the abuses by their poorly paid subordinates continued. Legitimate merchants complained of being held up at the customs barriers for days. They were outraged when women were searched and molested.

There were plenty of active smugglers, for the country was plagued by bands of *dacoits,* or robbers. The famine of 1770, coupled with the Company's ruthless collection of the land tax, had forced many former cultivators to take to crime. Moreover, the smugglers had immunity, for they were in league with the junior officers. A salt superintendent observed that he had 'never heard of a single seizure of sugar or smuggled salt'.

Similarly, the under-paid junior officers of the preventative *chowkies* abused their positions. No doubt their victims usually paid up quietly, but occasionally people complained, as they did of the Salt Officer of Baruipore, for:

1st – Throwing salt into the ryots' houses and arresting them on false charges of illicit manufacture, taking the said salt and earthen pots found about the premises as proof of the offence.

2ndly – Entering the ryots' habitations with 100 or 150 men in the night and apprehending all the inmates male and female and offering insults to the latter.

3rdly – Abstracting property from the ryots' houses while engaged in search for illicit salt.

4thly – Confinement at Cutcherry for 10 or 15 days and extracting confessions thereby.

The foundations were laid for a Customs Department that was to become a byword for corruption and extortion. In addition to paying the hated Salt Tax, the inhabitants of the Bengal Presidency were to be continually hindered, harassed and forced to pay bribes.

Of course, the unchecked smuggling did make some cheaper contraband salt available to the people. That was particularly true for those who lived on the borders of the Company's territory. Elsewhere, however, the smuggled salt was probably sold mixed with legal salt, and the merchants would have pocketed the difference. Contraband salt also often came from dubious sources, and there were many complaints of dirt and adulteration.

Despite the corruption in the salt department, the government was still able to collect vast amounts of Salt Tax. This was because they controlled, and could easily supervise, all the major salt works in Bengal. The *rowannah* and preventative *chowkies* may not have seized much contraband salt, but they did act as a deterrent to casual smuggling. Nevertheless, smuggling was an enormous problem for the government, and much effort would be expended on trying to eradicate it. It would become an even greater problem as the Company acquired new territories, and pushed its frontiers west to the borders of states rich in salt.

In 1801 the British forced the Nawab of Oudh to hand over half his dominions. This brought Rohilkhand, and the other northern districts between the River Ganges and the River Yamuna, under the control of the Company. The Maratha War of 1802–3 resulted in the acquisition of Delhi and Agra. All these lands became the North-Western Provinces of the Bengal Presidency. The Presidencies of Bengal and Madras became linked by further acquisitions, so that the entire eastern coast, and its salt-making capacity, became British. In 1818 the Marathas were finally crushed. Almost all of India, excepting Punjab and Sind, came under some degree of British control. A wide corridor of British territory linked the western districts of the Bengal Presidency to the Bombay Presidency.

There were still hundreds of Princely States, however, and these were only under indirect control. A British Resident gave 'advice' to the hereditary ruler, whose territories were liable to be seized if the advice were ignored. The rulers were free to raise their own taxes. Some of them taxed salt, and some did not. None taxed salt so heavily as the government of the Bengal Presidency. The Bengal Presidency, therefore, found itself bordered by princely territories with huge deposits of cheap salt. Moreover, it had acquired control of large populations who resented a sudden rise in the price of salt. Many of these areas were densely settled, had numerous roads and rivers, and were difficult to control. The *rowannah* and preventive *chowkies* which were erected in the newly acquired territories could not stem the flow of salt from the west.

In 1823 the Commissioner of Customs at Agra, George Saunders, suggested a new defence. He proposed that a secondary line of customs posts should be put on the trading routes running alongside the Yamuna River. It was this line of *chowkies* – rather than the haphazardly positioned original customs posts – which developed into the great Customs Line. Over the next fifty years, as the British took over more of India, the line would be moved many times. For a very short time it would be abandoned. Entirely separate sections would be started. Nevertheless, over the years, the Customs Line would grow inexorably longer and more formidable.

The original Customs Line ran from Mirzapur to Allahabad

along the south bank of the River Ganges, and then followed the Yamuna River to Agra. From there, it crossed open country, to end up just north-west of Delhi. This line controlled entry of salt into Bengal from the south and the west. There were, however, several complications and deficiencies. The tax on salt in Lower Bengal was half a rupee higher than that in North-Western Provinces. This necessitated customs barriers at Allahabad, and a line of customs posts running the few miles to the southern border and north all the way to Nepal. The Kingdom of Oudh formed an independent enclave within the Bengal Presidency. Until it was annexed in 1856, salt smuggling across its border was always a problem. Also, the north-western flank of the Bengal Presidency was unprotected. This was remedied, after the conquest of Sind and the Punjab in the 1840s, by extending the Customs Line north.

In 1834 G. H. Smith was appointed Commissioner of Customs. This had far-reaching consequences. Initially, Smith only had responsibility for the northern half of the Customs Line, but later he took control of the line in its entirety. He persuaded the government to exempt tobacco, iron, shawls and various other minor items from duty, and to concentrate its efforts on collecting the Salt Tax. He also initiated the abolition of the double line of customs posts. They were consolidated into a single line. In twenty years, Smith transformed the Customs Line from a series of individual customs posts into an effective barrier. When he retired in 1854 the annual budget for the Customs Line had grown to 790,000 rupees, and there was a staff of 6,600 men.

The upper part of the line – running from Agra past Delhi – was the first to be consolidated. *Chowkies* were erected one mile apart. Between the *chowkies*, the land was cleared, and a raised path made to join them. Each mile of the line was supervised by a *jemadar*, a non-commissioned officer, who had men posted every quarter of a mile. At night the men patrolled up and down their section. These duties alone, run on a shift system, required ten men for every mile. In addition, to apprehend smugglers who had already crossed the Customs Line, other patrols operated two or three miles inside it. Each guard had to sweep his section of the line when he took over, by trailing a large branch, or a special bamboo and grass frame, over the bare earth. This was inspected when he went off duty, and he was held responsible for any footsteps that crossed it.

As the Customs Line was solidified, it became an obstacle for those who lived in its vicinity. At first there was the minor irritant of having to run a gauntlet of aggressive customs officers on the make every time the line was crossed – perhaps to visit friends, or to tend land divided by the line. Later, journeys across the line became totally impractical. Large detours had to be made to go through one of its gateways, usually four miles apart.

In 1848, when the Raja of Satara died, he left an adopted son as his successor. Lord Dalhousie, the new Governor-General, arbitrarily decided that the state had lapsed to the Company, and seized it. Over the next few years the Doctrine of Lapse, backed by British military power, was used to assume control over many more states. Other states were invaded because the British thought them badly managed. The Bengal Presidency acquired huge new territories and populations from which to extract the Salt Tax.

The Mirzapur section of the line, which was no longer on the border of the Company's lands, was therefore abandoned. It had never been actively developed, and had relatively few guards. From a point a hundred miles down the Yamuna River from Agra, the Delhi–Agra section of the Customs Line was extended south for 350 miles, to encompass the newly conquered territories.

There was hardly time to adjust to these changes before the high-handed actions of the Company precipitated the great revolt of 1857, the 'Indian Mutiny'. This was only suppressed after a long and bitter campaign. Afterwards, the British government took over control of the country from the discredited East India Company and reorganised the administration. Rulers who had failed to support the British had their lands confiscated, and the Bengal Presidency expanded again. Nevertheless, the bizarre inequalities in the taxation of salt continued. Princely States still constituted much of India. They still taxed salt at a low rate, or not at all. The parts of British India controlled from Bombay and Madras continued to tax salt at a much lower rate than did the Bengal Presidency.

Following the further expansion of Bengal, the authorities in Calcutta were now in a position to construct one massive customs barrier. At first there were separate sections. After

various realignments, these were joined together in 1869 to make a continuous Customs Line. It was 2,504 miles long. It stretched from the foothills of the Himalayas to Orissa, and almost to the sea on the Bay of Bengal. The next ten years, from 1869 to 1879, saw the line reach an absurd perfection. An Inland Customs Department was established, with huge resources of men and money. The government considered the money well spent, for not only was tax collected on salt that crossed the Customs Line but, more importantly, the line deterred smuggling that would have ruined the government monopoly on the manufacture of salt. In 1869–70 the Salt Tax collected on the Customs Line was 12,500,000 rupees. The duty on salt imported by sea, and the profit on salt manufactured by the government, was another 30,000,000 rupees. In addition, duty on sugar as it left the Bengal Presidency raised another 1,000,000 rupees. That made a total of 43,500,000 rupees. The annual cost of the line was only 1,620,000 rupees. That was, nevertheless, a huge sum of money. The agricultural wage was still only about 3 rupees a month. It enabled the department to employ 12,000 men, and to construct a formidable barrier protected by 1,727 guard-posts.

The great Customs Line ran from Torbela, in the north of what is now Pakistan, down the east bank of the River Indus to Multan. That part of the line, however, was protected by the wide river, and only had occasional guard-posts. From Multan the heavily guarded line began. It was 1,428 miles long. It followed the north bank of the Sutlej River east to Fazilka, now just inside India. From there it ran south-east, keeping west of Delhi, then followed the south bank of the River Yamuna to Agra. It then turned south to Jhansi, Sagar, Hoshangabad and Khandwa, before terminating, on the present-day border between Madhya Pradesh and Maharashtra, just south of Burhanpur. The Customs Line then continued east, almost to the sea, for another 794 miles. However, as on the River Indus, this section only had occasional guard-posts and, as smuggling was minimal, was never considered important.

Like many great undertakings, the Customs Line reached perfection just before it became superfluous. The different rates of Salt Tax within British India had attracted much criticism. In 1869 the tax in Lower Bengal was 3.25 rupees a *maund*, and in the upper provinces 3 rupees. In Madras and Bombay it was only 1.9 rupees. The Customs Line, and its Customs Hedge, were expensive to maintain, and a major obstacle to travel and trade. In addition to the Salt Tax, there was also an export tax on sugar going to the Princely States. That resulted in obstructions to all traffic coming out of the Bengal Presidency, as well as to traffic going in. The customs officials harassed the population and extorted bribes. The barrier was a continual reminder of what Indians saw as unjust British taxes. Nevertheless, it continued to be strengthened.

While huge efforts were being made to bring the customs barrier to perfection, however, the government of India was planning its abolition. Under successive viceroys the possibilities of dismantling it were investigated, and steps taken to facilitate its demise. If the British could gain control of all salt production in India there would be no need for the Customs Line. If they could create a total monopoly, then the Salt Tax could be added on at the point of manufacture. The British already had control over salt production in their own territories; they needed to extend this over the Princely States.

Sambhar Salt Lake was the principal source of salt going into the Bengal Presidency from outside the Customs Line. This large lake – over twenty miles long – contracted in the dry season to leave vast quantities of salt lying on the dry ground. Large quantities of salt from there entered British India, either legally or smuggled. The lake was in the domains of the rulers of Jaipur and Jodhpur. Neither of them had used it as a source of revenue, and salt from there was cheap. By threat and bribery the British took over control of the lake. For the relatively small sum of 700,000 rupees a year, the rulers concluded the Salt Treaties that gave the British permanent leases over Sambhar and other salt works from 1 May 1871. They were fearful that the British might oust them if they did not comply. Nevertheless, they made little effort to protect their subjects, either from the ruin of their salt businesses, or the massive increases in the price of salt. Ram Singh, the ruler of Jaipur, did negotiate 170,000 *maunds* of cheap salt for his population. However, in 1879 he surrendered this for 400,000 rupees.

In 1878 A. O. Hume – who had earlier been Commissioner of Inland Customs, with responsibility for the Customs Line – was sent to conclude further salt agreements with the Princely States of Rajasthan. He was instructed to secure rights over the smaller salt sources. The Maharaja of Jaipur – who, for his services, had been made a member of the Legislative Council for British India – smoothed the way. The rulers of Jodhpur, Dholpur, Lawa, Bikaner, Sirohi, and Bharatpur, joined Jaipur in making salt agreements. Apart from a few minor caveats, they agreed to surrender all salt-manufacturing rights to the British. For a lump sum payment of 2,280,000 rupees – little more than the annual cost of maintaining the Customs Line – they delivered their subjects to a future of expensive salt. In effect, the inhabitants of Rajasthan would be paying the Salt Tax. However, because they did not live in British India, the Rajasthanis would receive no benefits from the taxation.

In 1876–8 another famine engulfed India. It was probably the worst in Indian history. It ravaged most of southern India, including Madras and Bombay, and then central India and the Punjab. In British India alone, at least six and a half million died. Huge areas of land were abandoned, and from there the land tax could not be collected. At the same time India was being pressured from Britain to remove the import tax on cotton goods. New sources of revenue had to be found. There was a comprehensive review of Indian taxation conducted by Sir John Strachey, long an advocate of abolishing the line.

In 1878 the government acted. The Salt Tax in the Bengal

Presidency was slightly reduced. Inside the Madras and Bombay Presidencies the Salt Tax was again increased. For all the people of British India, and many in the Princely States, cheap affordable salt disappeared. Small differences in the Salt Tax remained – it was 2.5 rupees in Madras, Bombay and north India, but 2.9 rupees in Lower Bengal – however not enough to make large-scale smuggling worth while. On 1 April 1879 the Customs Line was abandoned.

FIVE

Agra

Nothing beside remains. Round the decay
Of that colossal wreck, boundless and bare,
The lone and level sands stretch far away

P. B. SHELLEY, *Ozymandias*

In November 1997 I returned to India. I was sure that the detailed map of Agra I was carrying would lead me to the Customs Hedge, so sure, in fact, that I had spent my last day in England reading Max Hooper's book on the dating of hedges. I had wondered how 'Hooper's Hypothesis', which suggests that the number of extra species in a hedge is the same as its age in centuries, might adapt to India.

I flew into Delhi on a Saturday, and stayed once more with Didi. I had been looking forward to finding Santosh there, but he had been delayed in Gwalior. His mother had been sick with fever, so he had been looking after her. She was better, and he was expected next day. He arrived on Sunday evening, in high spirits, eager to resume our search.

75

In the morning we said farewell to Didi, who was taking the train to Jhansi later in the day, and went to New Delhi railway station to buy tickets. As I was going south after searching for the hedge, I had several to purchase. There was a special bureau for tourists. That could be very useful on heavily booked trains – often crowded out on national or school holidays, or for unpublicised local festivals – since there was a generous reserved quota of tickets for tourists. However, it is not possible to book extra tickets for Indian residents, so Santosh had to go off to the regular booking hall. As it happened, the tourist bureau was packed, so he was soon through, whereas I had to queue most of the day. Nevertheless, in the end we both successfully obtained reservations on the Shatabdi Express, which left early the next morning for Agra.

The train left at quarter past six, and we were in Agra two hours later. By chance, Didi had decided to break her journey overnight at Agra, before going on to Jhansi, and she was getting on to the Shatabdi as we were getting off. It was a fortuitous meeting, for she was able to introduce us to friends who were seeing her off. They insisted that we stay with them.

I had been worried about searching for the hedge in an area unfamiliar to Santosh. Wandering about people's fields with map and compass was a tricky business. Not unreasonably, they might suspect that we were interfering officials. Even worse, they might think we were spying. An Englishman was about to go on trial after a mysterious arms drop. Even though my map was dated 1879, my satellite navigator might cause suspicion. There was a general paranoia about spies in India, which was why no detailed modern maps were available to the public. Now, we had a wonderful introduction in SP, our host, who knew the whole area intimately. Although extremely well educated, and a college lecturer, he had been born into the shepherd caste and was active in helping his community. All the political parties were wooing his support. He had shepherd friends and connections throughout the region. Moreover, he had a nephew, Sachin, staying with him, who was keen to accompany us.

The family lived in West Agra. We unpacked and had lunch. Madhu, SP's wife, was from the Punjab, and we had the first of many delicious meals – *parathas* stuffed with potatoes and chillies, and served with yoghurt. Afterwards, we went on a sightseeing expedition to the tomb of Akbar, the Mughal emperor, a few miles to the north-west. As a forerunner of the Taj Mahal, I found the mausoleum interesting, but I had another reason for the visit – I wanted to re-set my satellite navigator, and check the reading against the old map.

At first I thought something was wrong with the machine, for the longitude it gave was considerably different to that on the map. It was only when I returned to the house that I realised the error was with the map. I could have discovered the inaccuracy in London, if I had bothered to check. I had been so impressed by its professional appearance and detail, that it had never occurred to me that the latitude and longitude might not be correct. A glance at my American aeronautical chart, which showed the 78° East line as passing through Agra, whereas it was well to the west on the old map, highlighted the discrepancy. There was a difference of several miles. Fortunately, the longitude looked about right.

I read off the satellite fix for Akbar's tomb and compared it with the 1879 map. The latitude was spot on. The longitude, on the other hand, was out by three minutes of a degree, or about three miles. I swore, as I remembered the hours I had spent working out co-ordinates to a hundredth of a minute. I had hoped to be accurate to within a hundred yards – a reasonable distance from which to spot the hedge. An error of three miles seemed to make the map impossible to use in conjunction with the satellite navigator.

During the night, while I slept, the problem partly resolved itself. I awoke more cheerful. It seemed probable to me that the error had been caused by a defective chronometer. In order to determine longitude, it had been necessary for the Victorians to compare local time, as indicated by the sun, with Greenwich Mean Time. That had needed extraordinarily accurate watches, set to the time in Greenwich. Any error would be replicated on to the map. With any luck the error would be a constant one, and I could recalculate the co-ordinates. On our first trip to look for the Customs Hedge, we could go to a nearby landmark and check to see if the inaccuracy was constant.

SP was driving to Delhi next day. He offered to make a detour and drop us off before he went north, at the village of Jakhoda about six miles due south of Agra. I had chosen Jakhoda because, on the map, it was where the hedge met the line of the Delhi and Agra Canal. There was a horseshoe bend in the canal at that point, too. If it still existed, it should help pinpoint the spot.

Jakhoda was easy to travel to. It was a couple of miles off the main road to Gwalior, and lay near a tarred road that, judging by the number of lorries on it, served as a bypass around Agra. This narrow road ran alongside a huge ditch, which was obviously the dried-up relic of the Delhi and Agra Canal. It was reassuring to see that it had not been obliterated by time. The horseshoe bend was still there. The village, of perhaps a hundred houses, was over a bridge, then a few hundred yards south of the old canal.

SP introduced us to the head of the village and explained about the hedge. The *sarpanch* had no knowledge of its whereabouts, but was happy for us to search over the village fields. SP wished us luck and drove off. I switched on my GPS navigator. I was pleased to see that the latitude was the same as on the map, and the longitudinal inaccuracy exactly what I expected.

We set off to find the hedge. My young companions looked unlikely explorers. City teenagers, they wore jeans, neatly pressed shirts and smart shoes. Santosh had a trendy denim jacket; Sachin his biker's leather jacket and pointed sunglasses. Only I, or so I fondly imagined, was dressed appropriately – in faded khaki and jungle hat. However, it was I who found the going tough under the strong sun as we plodded across the fields. The wheat had already been harvested, giving a good clear view. The land was flat, perfectly so, as was necessary for the flood irrigation system that covered the entire area. It was obvious that in the recent past there had been a major construction of ditches and dykes. The landscape had been totally altered. Here and there the fields were bordered by hedges, but they were insubstantial and short. I set my compass to the line of the old Customs Hedge. There was no sign of any trees or shrubs running off in that direction.

The railway line from Agra to Gwalior was only a mile to the east. I thought that perhaps, if I could find the spot where the Customs Hedge crossed it, some remnants of the hedge might be left in the uncultivated strip beside the line. We walked along the road that led to the railway, then climbed up the embankment on to the track. With my satellite navigator in my hand, I walked north until I reached the calculated intersection with the Customs Line. We were high above the surrounding land, so we could see far in every direction. We studied the shrub-covered land beside the railway. We scanned the nearby fields. We walked up and down the railway lines, in case we were not at the exact crossing point. There was absolutely no sign of the Customs Hedge. It was a terrible morning for me. I had been quite sure we would find some remains. The map was so detailed, that success had seemed inevitable. But all my dreams had evaporated. I was devastated.

It was noon, and hot. On the edge of a nearby field of sugar

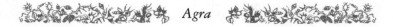

cane, a tractor drove a crushing mill. Two brick vats, six feet across and three feet deep, were full of steaming juice. Crushed cane fed a fire below. From an adjacent thatched shelter, the proprietor, clad in immaculate white Nehru jacket and trousers, watched the boiling vats with satisfaction. He and his two labourers were making *ghur* – blocks of crude brown sugar.

He gestured for us to join him. We sat down in the shade, while one of the men fetched fresh juice straight from the crusher. It was not so sweet as I had feared and, as the sugar coursed through me, almost instantly reviving.

We walked back along the road, then crossed the bridge over the old canal into the village. The *sarpanch* invited us to lunch. As the meal was being cooked, he took us on a tour of the village. He was rightly proud of many recent improvements. Raised brick roads and drainage canals had been constructed, to make life easier in the rainy season. However, any major changes were a long way off, for they received virtually no help from the government. Despite being so near a good road, they still had no clinic, no post office and no electricity. We had a tasty lunch of spiced vegetables, *dal* and *rotis,* then rested. As usual, I found it difficult to arrange my tall thin body on the annoyingly short *charpoy* – the ubiquitous bed of plaited hemp. My mind was full of our failure. Nevertheless, I nodded off and slept for an hour.

We thanked our host, who seemed genuinely sorry at our lack of success, and set off to walk back to the main Gwalior to Agra road. From there we could get transport back to Agra.

We left the village with directions to take a different route, a hundred yards to the east, which crossed the old dried-up canal by another bridge. We had not realised there were two ways into the village. As we approached the bridge, I switched on my satellite navigator. We were almost exactly on the line where the Customs Hedge would have crossed the canal. I became excited when I saw that the little bridge was of old brick. In the centre of the parapet was a terracotta plaque. It was inscribed 'Jakhoda 1873'.

I felt sure this was where the road, which ran alongside the hedge, had crossed the old canal. The date was right. The position was right. However, hard as I looked, I could see nothing significant beyond the bridge. The road, and its Customs Hedge, had been totally obliterated. We walked beside the canal, until we hit the main road. According to my calculations we were only half a mile north of where the hedge had run. We turned south along the edge of the highway, dodging the careering buses and trucks, and looked to the east and to the west. There was nothing to be seen.

'Don't worry,' Santosh said, 'we're bound to find the hedge eventually.'

'Of course we are,' I replied, and smiled. But I was not hopeful.

Over the next few days we made forays into other areas close to the line of the Customs Hedge. We traversed the twenty miles of the Customs Line that ran east from Jakhoda to the edge of the map, near Fatehabad. The only encouragement we had was about halfway along, at Shamshabad.

Shamshabad was small on the 1879 map, and still small in 1997. There were just a few buildings running along a road, which were surrounded by open fields. That made it easy to get a satellite bearing from the old centre, then walk north. We weaved along the edges of the fields. Every few minutes we had to stop to explain ourselves to farmers. They were interested in the story of the Salt Tax and the Customs Hedge, and we quizzed them in vain for any memories or information, so progress was slow. Eventually, when we were a mile and a half due north of Shamshabad, I took out my compass and lined it up with the route of the hedge. I looked to the east and to the west, but there were only bare fields with their random hedges and trees. I decided to follow the line easterly, to where it should have intersected the Agra to Shamshabad road.

It was a beautiful clear day, and not too hot, so it was impossible to be downhearted. Iridescent birds flapped along the green hedges; peacocks ran off across the bare fields. At one time I became excited when I saw a fort-like building, thinking it might be one of the old customs posts. We found the farmer, who looked at us rather oddly, before assuring us it had been built as a store by his father. As we approached the main road, the concentration of hedges and copses increased.

We found ourselves walking between two rows of hedges, about twenty yards apart. The narrow ploughed strip was hedged with very large trees on the north side, and smaller trees to the south. It was exactly aligned with the hedge on the map. However, it only ran for about a hundred yards, and the large trees had no thorns. I was not convinced.

So, after a week in Agra, all we had found was a bridge and a dubious line of trees. It was extremely disappointing. Intensive farming had obliterated the Customs Hedge. However, I did not intend to give up. I would have to look for an area that was less heavily cultivated.

I had the map of Jhansi District. It was eight miles to the inch. Would the detail be enough? Would there be sections that had not been destroyed by cultivation? I was committed to accompanying Santosh back to Gwalior, and spending a few days with him before we parted. I had also arranged to make a quick visit to friends in southern India. I decided, therefore, to adjust my return itinerary from the south, so that before I caught my flight in Delhi, I would have a few days in Jhansi District. On my own, with the poor map I had, I was not too hopeful that I would find anything. However, I would be able to see how heavily the land was cultivated, and decide whether it would be worth while to hunt for a better map.

We made a short visit to Vrindavan, a temple-town associated with Lord Krishna, to visit friends. Then Santosh and I went on to Gwalior for a hectic few days. I bloated myself on too many sumptuous meals, and between-meals impossible-to-refuse snacks and sweets. His family and friends were eager to hear of our adventures. I had some of my photographs hurriedly developed, and showed them around. To save Santosh's feelings, I put an optimistic gloss on our failures. Everyone urged us to continue the search.

I said farewell to Santosh, promising to meet up with him when I next returned to India, then took the train south to Bangalore. There my friends came from a very different background. I toured pubs, accompanied by artists and highly qualified scientists. Afterwards, I went to a Krishna festival, at Udipi, on the south-west coast; then back inland to the magnificent ruins at Hampi, set in a fantastic bouldered landscape. Finally, I made a fourteen-hour bus journey to see friends of friends at Hyderabad. Then, I caught the train back north to Jhansi.

It would have been easier to search for the hedge from Jhansi itself. However, I found it a dirty and depressing town, so I took a *tempo* to Orcha, ten miles south-east. Even though it had quadruple its proper load of five passengers, it successfully negotiated the badly potholed road.

Orcha, a small town on an island in the Betwa River, had been abandoned by its raja in the eighteenth century. It had become a backwater of crumbling palaces. The largest, the Jhagangir Mahal, was a seventeenth-century extravaganza,

built to commemorate the emperor's visit. It had a multitude
of domes, balconies, arches and courtyards. Vultures nested in
the turrets. There were also a few rooms where you could stay,
so I moved in. Facing the palace, a humped stone bridge led to
a small bazaar with a couple of travellers' restaurants, and then
on to temples and more palaces. I spent the rest of the day
looking round the small town, chatting to long-stay travellers, and avoiding a noisy group of marigold-garlanded
British tourists.

My 1874 map of Jhansi District showed the Customs Line
running from Jhansi south towards Lalitpur. Since the scale
was only eight miles to the inch, there was not much detail. It
seemed, however, that the line ran close to the present road for
a dozen miles, as far as Khailar. Then there was a diversion. It
turned sharply south-west for about seven miles, before
turning back to join the road again at Babina, and then follow
it on to Lalitpur.

Where the road and the Customs Line were close, I reasoned,
there would be little chance of finding the hedge. The old road
used to maintain the Customs Hedge could well have been
widened, destroying any remnants in the process. The deviation, on the other hand, which had probably followed the
boundary of a Princely State, might have been left undisturbed.
The Customs Hedge might still be there. I went to bed early,
planning to start the search first thing in the morning, and
prayed that the land would be relatively uncultivated.

I awoke to heavy fog. The palaces in the town were
completely hidden.

'When will it clear?' I asked the watchman.

'We don't normally get weather like this in November,' he replied, drawing a heavy blanket tighter round his shoulders and pulling down a woolly hat, 'so who can say?'

By ten o'clock, the fog had lifted enough to see the top of the turret high above my room. The vultures sat huddled, unable to find the thermals they needed to fly and search for food. I packed a bag for the day, and wandered into the bazaar to take a *tempo* to Jhansi. Khailar was actually only six miles west of Orcha, but there was no road. I needed to go north to Jhansi, and then travel back south again. I found a *tempo* just ready to depart – lucky, because they did not follow a timetable, but only left when full, or over-full. Packed tightly together, we kept reasonably warm in the doorless three-wheeler.

The fog was even thicker in Jhansi. It was impossible to see across the bus station. I peered at the bus destinations, trying to decipher the Hindi characters. Things were not made easier by everyone assuming that an Englishman was looking, not for a bus to Khailar but, like most foreigners, for one going to the erotic sculptures at Khajuraho.

'Khailar?' I enquired, aware that my pronunciation was probably not good, but nevertheless becoming more and more ill-tempered. 'Khailar?'

'Yes, yes,' conductors enthused, dragging me on to their buses. 'Khajuraho.'

Eventually, I found a bus going to Lalitpur, via Khailar. Five miles out of Jhansi the fog suddenly dispersed. I was doubly cheered to see a landscape dotted with hills, and only occasionally cultivated. At Khailar, the road ran between rocky scrub-covered hills. I was the only person to get off at the short ribbon of roadside shops. I bought a glass of tea at a stall. People looked at me quizzically.

I was somewhat nervous about wandering across the countryside on my own. In Agra, assisted by Santosh, and with political patronage, I had encountered no problems. Here, however, I was on my own. With my electronic navigator and compass, I might easily be thought to be a spy. I focused on an elderly man in a smart Nehru jacket. In broken Hindi, I explained my quest. Explanations were made difficult by the lack of an exact Hindi word for hedge. The nearest equivalent, *baar,* could mean any kind of fence. Fortunately the old man, and the crowd that pressed round, seemed to understand the gist of what I said. They were friendly.

I took out my satellite navigator to get a fix. The villagers asked if it was a mobile telephone. I was in the middle of explaining what the machine really was, pushing my Hindi to the limit, when a motorbike screeched to a halt.

'Is that a GPS?' a young leather-jacketed Indian asked, in perfect English.

'You've seen one before?'

'Yes, I'm in computers with the army. What are you doing?'

I explained about the Salt Tax and the Customs Hedge. He seemed quite unsurprised. He then explained everything in detail to the villagers. They also seemed unsurprised, and not very interested. No one knew of such a hedge, but I was welcome to go and look for it. The young man wrote out his phone number, and asked for my address in England.

'Give me a ring if you need help with the GPS.' He glanced at my card, put it away, and started to move off. 'I'll send you an e-mail to see how you got on.'

The map showed the Customs Line heading east, away from the road just south of Khailar, at 243°. I walked south along the road, until I was past all the buildings. I scanned the land to my right – to the east. There were some fields, but most of the land was unfarmed. Then, I saw a raised bank, thirty feet high, beginning close to the road and heading off in approximately the right direction. Excited, and remembering that there had been mention in the Annual Reports of some of the hedge being raised, I ran up the bank. I found myself looking into a wide irrigation canal.

However, the canal did go off vaguely in the right direction, so I followed the path on one of its banks. I had an excellent view of the surrounding land. I calculated that I should cross the Customs Line when my satellite navigator showed a bearing back to Khailar of 117°. That would be several miles away, but it seemed a good plan. Away from the village there would probably be less cultivation, and less destruction of trees for firewood. As I walked eastwards, I kept an eye on the navigator. The land was almost deserted. Occasionally, I passed a goatherd and exchanged greetings, or waved to an isolated farmer cultivating a fertile patch of soil. Very slowly, as I moved further east, the bearing back to Khailar increased. After two miles, though, it was only 60°. Moreover, the canal was turning south, whereas I needed to go north to increase the angle. I climbed down the embankment, waded through a stream, and followed such little footpaths through the scrub as took me north.

I was pleased to see no sign of cultivation, for that made the survival of the Customs Hedge more likely. It occurred to me that I was taking a risk, travelling alone, far from habitation. No one would hear me if I encountered robbers, which were quite common in such remote areas. Soon, however, the landscape became more fertile. There were fields and occasional houses. I was almost 117° from Khailar. Then I saw a railway – the line from Jhansi to Lalitpur. I climbed up the embankment to get a better view. There was very little cultivation on the other side of the line, to the west. It was mostly coarse grass and small shrubs. I climbed back down, and resumed walking. I crossed the 117° line, and avidly scanned the landscape. There was no sign of a hedge.

A cyclist came by, a sack of wheat on his handlebars. He stopped to greet and to quiz me. I explained what I was doing.

'You shouldn't be here,' he said.

'Why not?'

'Robbers,' he said, patting his breast pocket.

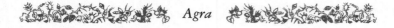

He rode off, and I was left feeling rather nervous. There was little point in continuing now that I had crossed the estimated line of the Customs Hedge. I decided to walk a couple of hundred yards more, to allow for errors, and then turn back.

Suddenly, a villainous-looking man, complete with bandit-like moustache, and waving a sickle, leapt out from behind a bush. I froze. He stared at me, then burst into laughter.

'*Namaste,*' he said. 'I heard you were on your way. Come to the village, and tell us about the English hedge.'

Only a few minutes' walk away, hidden by trees, there was a small village. I followed my imitation bandit into the compound that enclosed his tiny house. Children rushed to peer at us over the mud wall. A dozen men came in to join us. I was offered a seat on a *charpoy* and was soon drinking water from the well, eating *dal* and *chapatis*, and explaining about the Customs Hedge. There was much interest, but no one could offer any useful information. Despondent, I walked back to Khailar.

In Orcha that evening there was plenty of activity. Some local politicians had come to visit the Ram Raja Temple. In complete contrast to the weathered stone elsewhere, it was painted bright pink. An old palace, it had been used as a temporary shrine for a statue of Ram brought from Ayodhya.

Later, when the statue resisted all efforts to move it, the palace had been converted into a temple. The politicians arrived in style. They were in two gleaming white four-wheel-drive Sumos, and escorted by numerous vehicles, carrying police and party men. In addition to the police, they had personal bodyguards with light machine guns.

I sat outside one of the little restaurants nearby, eating *pakoras* and surveying the spectacle. An amusing old Austrian couple kept up a barrage of *sotto voce* cynical remarks about the humility of politicians. I smiled, but my mind was elsewhere. I could not see how I had failed to find any sign of the hedge that afternoon. Of course, the map was small scale, and not very detailed. Unlike at Agra, however, the land was relatively uncultivated. There had been plenty of old trees and short runs of ancient hedges. Why had none of them been even vaguely on the right bearing?

Depressed, I ordered myself a double banana pancake. The politicians left, and the town became quiet again. Shops began to close. I paid my bill and walked back towards my room in the old palace. On the sixteenth-century bridge, I suddenly realised where I might have gone wrong. My figures had probably been based on a fundamental navigational error. I hurried back to my room, took out the map and instruments, and began to check my calculations.

As soon as I looked at a protractor, I saw I was right. For some reason, I had calculated the reverse bearing of 243° – the line of the hedge out of Khailar – as 117°. I had subtracted 243° from 360°, which seemed logical, but was wrong.

Laying a ruler across the protractor, I could see that opposite from 243° was 63°. From 243°, I should have subtracted 180°. It was obvious, and I should have realised, that the hedge ran north-east, and not south-east, back to Khailar. I had so concentrated on my satellite navigator that I had ignored common sense. The real bearing of the hedge back to Khailar was 63°.

It was clear that most of the walking I had done from Khailar had been useless. I needed to return the next day and try again. I now knew that the terrain, and its general lack of cultivation, gave hope. Surely, now that I had discovered my error, there was a good chance of finding the hedge. I prepared for an early start, and slept soundly.

I awoke at dawn, stiff from the previous day's long and unnecessary walk. There was a thin mist. I took a *tempo* to Jhansi, and then a bus to Khailar. When we arrived, the sky had completely cleared. The man with the tea stall recognised me, and called me over. I drank the sweet milky tea. Declining the offer of a fly-covered cake, I set off south. Just out of the village, I climbed once again on to the embankment of the canal, and took out my compass. I now saw that the canal ran almost exactly at 243°. It was either right on top of the Customs Hedge, or on a closely parallel line. I walked along, examining the country on either side. Nothing obvious stood out.

I walked to where the canal turned south. There, instead of going north, as I had the day before, I climbed down and went straight ahead. The land was sandy and uncultivated.

Occasional bushes dotted the coarse grass. Nowhere was there a proper line of trees or shrubs. I walked for another two miles, until I reached the railway embankment again. On the other side the landscape was similar. I scanned the horizon, but it did not look hopeful. Suddenly, the sound of heavy guns rolled towards me. There was an artillery range ahead. It would have been foolish to proceed further. I surveyed the landscape one last time, sighed, and then turned back.

Close to Khailar, looking down from the canal embankment, I did see a short length of a field boundary hedge running parallel to the canal. I climbed down, then went across country to examine it. Some of the trees, although cut short, were definitely old. What was more, I recognised acacia trees and Indian plum. I gingerly took hold of a trailing acacia branch. The paired white needle-like spikes, which stood out from the base of each leaf stalk, were fully two inches long. They were extremely hard to break. The Indian plum shrubs had thorns too. These were much shorter, but also occurred in pairs. Rather peculiarly, one was straight, and the other hooked. The hedge was sparsely planted and, as an experiment, I tried to gently force my way through. Almost immediately, I was caught up in the thorns. It was easy to see that the much thicker Customs Hedge would have been 'utterly impassable'.

Nearby some farmers were harvesting peanuts. They waved at me to come over. We sat in their little thatch shelter, eating nuts and drinking tea. I told them about my search, and asked about the adjacent hedge. They had no idea of how old it might be, but doubted that it had been part of a much longer barrier.

Beyond Khailar, to the east, there was a conical hill. It was maybe 500 feet high, with a ruin on top. I walked to the centre of town, then turned off the main road down an alley. To my surprise it was lined with beautiful old houses faced in blue plaster. They had ornate carved doors and balconies, and crenellated walls. The children playing outside followed me into the fields beyond. They led me up the hill to the little ruined temple on top. There was a panoramic view of the countryside. I switched my GPS navigator on to a fix I had made at Orcha, and set my compass on the bearing. I was thrilled to see, right on the hairline, the domes of the Jhagangir Mahal. It was the only triumph of the day, for there was nothing else to be seen. Surrounded by happy children, I trudged back to the village and waited for a bus. It would be another year before I could return to resume the search.

The Customs Hedge

No one who has not taken in hand the cultivation of a
thousand miles of live hedge . . . can form any conception
of the Herculean labour this involves.

ALLAN OCTAVIAN HUME, Commissioner of Inland Customs

It is not known exactly when the live Customs Hedge was first established, but it was almost certainly in the 1840s. Similarly, it is impossible to say who first had the idea of making the customs barrier a live green hedge. G. H. Smith, who was Commissioner of Customs from 1834 to 1854 wrote:

In the performance of their preventative duties, the establishment are aided in many beats by a thick, horny hedge, composed of bya [briar?] bushes, and raised sufficiently high to prevent its being surmounted without being broken through, and so creating an alarm which speedily brings the men on duty in the vicinity of the spot. On some parts of the line, the patrols have commenced sowing a live hedge, and others have in

97

contemplation to adopt the same plan, so that in the course of a few years we may calculate upon having an impenetrable and permanent barrier to head-load smuggling across a large portion of the North-west frontier line.

Another customs officer recorded that 'It happened at the first instance to spring up by chance.' Presumably this occurred when part of the cut thorn-bush barrier took root. We know, from official reports, that by 1854 the hedge was energetically taking root. By 1868, the Commissioner of Inland Customs, Allan Octavian Hume, could write, 'I reckon that there are 180 miles only, at the present moment, of *thoroughly* impenetrable live hedge in existence.' One hundred and eighty miles only!

Some idea of how enormous the labour was of maintaining it can be found in Hume's report for the year 1867–8 on the North-Western Provinces section of the Customs Line:

Very considerable improvements have been effected in the hedge during the past year. At the present moment, throughout the Muttra, Agra, and some three-fourths of the Jhansie divisions, a good hedge, live or dry, presents, as a whole, a nearly impassable barrier to smugglers. Local accidents, however, continually weaken the dry hedge; storms overthrow a mile at a time; the mis-directed labour of colonies of white ants, suddenly result in large gaps; sometimes even, portions catch or are set on fire; day by day, the work at the hedge continues, and no one out of the department at all realises the incredible amount of labour that even 200 miles of good dry hedge (and we have more than this in this division) represents.

It is calculated that every mile of good hedge requires 250 tons of material, and it is a very low estimate if we allot 50,000 tons to the dry hedge of the North-West Provinces Section. All this, cut by the establishment (in some cases at no little risk of collision with villagers), carried by them from distances of from one-fourth to even *five* and *six* miles, and staked in its place. It is not too much to say that what with decay, white ants, fires and storms, at least half has to be renewed yearly.

Elsewhere in the same report are details of the lengths of dry hedge running both north and south of the North-Western Provinces. These doubled the total length of the dry hedge, so that taken all together 'the men have cut, carried and stacked on it fully 100,000 tons of thorny brushwood'. The next year it was reported that over 150,000 tons of thorny material were collected and carried into position.

It was this phenomenal labour requirement that gave impetus to the establishment of the live hedge. In his report for 1869–70, his final year as Commissioner, Hume noted:

With the dry hedge, our labour is as that of Sisyphus,

ceaseless and, beyond the immediate moment, resultless. Whereas a live hedge, although for the first few years entailing, where soil or climate are adverse, an absolutely inconceivable amount of labour and trouble, if once reared, thereafter needs only ordinary care. Except, therefore, where we cross bare solid rock, a live hedge is what we aim at, but no one who has not taken in hand the cultivation of a thousand miles of live hedge, stretching over a vast continent, where soil and climate are not only variable in the extreme, but, as in our case, too often adverse to a degree to any line of continuous vegetation, can form any conception of the Herculean labour this involves.

A great variety of experiments have been tried; almost every description of locally indigenous thorny shrubs has been tried, wherever peculiar difficulties were experienced. Many tons of the best seeds have been systematically and carefully collected by the men, under the immediate supervision of their officers. Sowings have been repeated, not once, but a dozen times, on different systems. Where water from wells or other sources was absolutely unprocurable and the soil very arid, long trenches have been dug and attempts made to store the rain water. Where floods yearly rotted the young plants, as they did throughout long stretches of Jhansie and Saugor, many miles of broad ridges have been raised on which to sow the seed. Many miles of bank have again been thrown up for the growth of the prickly pear in places like Urneewalla (Hissar), where nothing else will grow. In many places stony ground has been thickly coated with, and in others barren soil dug out and replaced by, good earth brought from a distance.

I have dwelt somewhat at length on this subject, unreasonably so, it may, I fear, be thought, but I believe that on no branch of their duties have the whole establishment bestowed anything like so much time, labour, care, and thought, as on the rearing of this barrier, of which all admit the paramount necessity, while regretting the ceaseless and painful toil it entails; and after all it must be remembered that our barrier is to the LINE what the Great wall once was to China, alike its greatest work and its chiefest safeguard.

In his previous annual report, the Commissioner had written:

Great progress has been made in defending our line by an impenetrable barrier. The hedge in every beat has been closely examined and measured, and we prove to have altogether 448¾ miles of *perfect* hedge, and 233½ miles of hedge which, though strong and good, requires future additions to render it impenetrable. This hedge is in places solely a live hedge, in others entirely a dry, thorny barrier; while in others, again, it is a combination of the two. The hedge is nowhere less than eight feet high and four to five feet thick; but in places it is as much as twelve feet high and fourteen feet thick at the bottom.

In the three years, 1867–70, A. O. Hume transformed the Customs Hedge. Inheriting 'a mere line of persistently dwarf seedlings, or of irregularly scattered, disconnected bushes', he left behind 682¼ miles of good hedge. Hume had quickly realised that, with the Customs Line running through such different terrain, more than one strategy was needed:

In some places bamboos are found to answer beyond all expectations; in others, digging a deep trench and mixing better earth with the soil of the place, promises to succeed. In some places, a low narrow bank of earth thrown up, has furnished a thriving row of young plants, where excess of water has previously destroyed all the seedlings. The prickly pear (*Opuntia*) is found, in places, to succeed rapidly. Nothing but local experience and discrimination, based on a consideration of the physical conditions of each locality, will help us. System is absolutely necessary, but not of that nature that would generalise a single plan for such diverse climates and soils.

All was not only extension and infilling, for during Hume's tenure the Customs Line was substantially realigned. The various separate sections were joined together into one continuous line. Troublesome gaps and spurs were eliminated. Whole sections of the existing Customs Hedge were abandoned, and new sections were established from scratch. In his first report Hume wrote of the Bengal Presidency:

> An area of five hundred thousand square miles and a population of one hundred and thirty millions may be approximately assigned to this vast tract; and to *aid* the realisation of the tax on the *whole* of the salt consumed within this tract, by levying an import duty along its entire land frontier, is the principal object of the Imperial Customs Line.

By 1870 it seemed that this objective was close to being achieved. Hume, with his ornate phrases and passion for detail, would be rewarded with promotions, until he became Secretary to the Government of India.

The next Commissioner, from 1870 to 1876 was G. H. M. Batten. Until his last year in office, there was very little further realignment of the Customs Line, and he concentrated on making the existing line impregnable. Where it was impossible to grow a green hedge because of the barrenness of the country, or even stake out one of dry thorn, he adopted new measures. In some places a ditch and mound were dug. In others a stone wall was built. Batten's main concern, however, was to extend and consolidate the Customs Hedge. There was much still to do. At the end of his first year Batten reported:

> The perfect barrier has increased by $111\frac{1}{4}$ miles. On the Sutledge line alone 24 miles of perfect protection, and $120\frac{1}{2}$ miles of less perfect protection, by a dry hedge, has been provided in the course of the year. In the Hissar Division the insufficient barrier is chiefly in the northern beats, but there is a ditch and mound which gives great security from Fazilika to Ladwi. The Dilhi Division is completely protected except for two miles. The prickly pear (nagphani) seems to succeed here. In the Agra Division the barrier is now perfect throughout, half being live hedge. In the Jhansie Division there have been great difficulties to contest with. Frost and field rats attacked the young plants. With regard to the rats, the Collector reports 'the Patrol of Chirgaon has let loose a number of wild cats in his hedge, whose presence has cleared the place of these destructive animals to some extent.' It will be observed that in this division there are three-quarters of a mile of stone wall.
>
> In the Sagar Division there is a mile and three-quarters of stone wall. The Collector gives a very unfavourable account of the protection afforded by the hedge; in almost every beat there are portions which, being insufficient, nullify the advantages of the perfect hedge where it exists.

The Collector has called the attention of his subordinates to this most important matter, and I hope to find great improvements in the current year. In the Hoshungabad Division the hedge nowhere forms a perfect barrier. The soil for the upper ten miles of the division is very bad. The only plant likely to thrive is cactus, of which nurseries are being made. There are fifteen miles of better but still bad soil in the Burhanpur Section. To the eastwards where a hedge is most essential there is a good promise of its being in time efficient. In the Nagpur Division there is no hedge, and luckily is not much required, as there is little smuggling. In the Raipur Division the efforts to make a live hedge have everywhere failed.

It seems that a decision was made not to develop the hedge in the Raipur Division. It was terminated (at what is now the border between Madhya Pradesh and Maharashtra) just south of Burhanpur. That was to be the final limit of the hedge. Until its demise the Customs Hedge ran from Burhanpur roughly north – via Khandwa, Hoshangabad, Sagar, Jhansi, Jalaun, Agra, Mathura, Rohtak, Hissar, and Fazilka. At Fazilka (where it crossed into what is now Pakistan) it turned east to Pakpattan, Jalalpur, and the confluence of the Rivers Sutlej and Chenab. Finally it turned north again and followed the east bank of the River Indus to end at Leia. Above Leia the current on the Indus was considered strong enough to deter smugglers without the need for a hedge, but there were patrols along the riverbank and the ferries were controlled.

The total length of the hedge, green and dry, in March 1873, should have been 1,248 miles. In fact, there were gaps both in the north and in the south. In the centre, the Agra and Delhi Divisions had been made almost impregnable but only after much effort. The Collector of the Agra Division reported:

> White ants will attack large and vigorous looking trees, causing them to dry up and decay; the hot winds often blast a number of them, making an unsightly gap where none existed a short time before; parasital creepers, if not watched, will envelope and blight a length of the hedge, leaving us no remedy but complete eradication of the trees attached ere we can destroy the pests; locusts will, as in 1872–73, settle in the hedge, and, if they do no worse, check its growth; and finally, we have the natural decay of the trees to encounter, keeping us continually planting and transplanting without cessation or intermission. In 1872–73 we had one more scourge in the shape of an Assistant Revenue Surveyor in the Bah Pinahat Tahsil of the Agra division, who, before I could communicate with his superior, had cut gaps in the Bah and Tathiabad beats in four places at his will and pleasure, destroying wantonly what it has cost us, of all grades, years of labour to rear and bring to perfection.

However, as the Commissioner observed on this tale of woe: 'Notwithstanding all this, the hedge in the greater part of the

Agra Division flourishes to such a height and thickness as to be, if not "a thing of beauty", a standing monument of the industry of our officers and men and an impervious barrier to smugglers.'

The Agra Canal, taking irrigation water from the River Yamuna near Delhi, opened in 1874. In 1875–6, G. H. M. Batten's last year as Commissioner, the Customs Line in the Agra Division was moved to run beside the almost parallel new canal. It only involved a realignment of a mile or two either side of the old line. Nevertheless, his staff would not have been pleased, for he decided to abandon the by then almost perfect hedge, and to grow another along the canal bank. Because of the effectiveness of the canal as a barrier, the distance between guard-posts was increased from half a mile to one and a half miles, so this had to be achieved with a reduced workforce.

The last Commissioner to take control of the Customs Hedge was W. S. Halsey. In his first two years the hedge reached its greatest extent and perfection. In one year alone, in the Agra District, sixty-two miles of hedge was planted to a width of fourteen feet. Halsey's reports were shorter, less full of description, and more prosaic than those of his predecessors. However, he was given to compiling meticulous tables, which

analysed in great detail. His report for 1877–8 recorded the
state of the customs barrier:

'Perfect' and 'Good'– Green Hedge	411.50 miles
– Combined Green	
and Dry Hedge	298.15 miles
– Dry Hedge	471.75 miles
– Stone Wall	6.35 miles
'Wanting' and 'Insufficient'	333.25 miles
Total	1,521.00 miles

That part of the Line 'wanting' a barrier was entirely in the
Punjab North, where the rivers gave good protection. The
'insufficient' barrier was mostly in the Punjab South and the
Central Provinces. Only three miles of barrier in the smug-
gler- beset North-Western Provinces were below standard.
The 'perfect' and 'good' green hedge, sometimes backed up by
a dry-thorn one, was over 700 miles long. It can be assumed
that at least a hundred miles of the 'insufficient' barrier was a
substantial, if not impregnable, green hedge. In the final
years, then, the green hedge was at least 800 miles long.

Halsey's very same report, however, also announced the
termination of this extraordinary endeavour. With one
sentence he announced the end. 'In conclusion,' he wrote, 'I
may remark that generally all expenditure in the repair of the
live hedge has been stopped in view of the approaching aboli-

tion of the Inland Customs Line.' A year later the entire Customs Line and its great hedge lay abandoned.

The Customs Line required a huge army of officers and men. In 1869 there were 136 officers, 2,499 petty officers, and 11,288 men – a total workforce of 13,923, and it was still expanding. Establishing the hedge was only part of the job. As Hume wrote that year:

> It is difficult to convey, either in words or figures, the immense amount of work done during the year by our officers and men as a body. To say our officers marched and patrolled 350,000 miles, and weighed over 200,000 tons of goods, and the men walked over 18,000,000 of miles, dug over 2,000,000 of cubic feet of earth in connection with trenches and banks of the new green hedge, collected and carried over 150,000 tons of thorny material for the dry hedge, and so on, sounds like one of the arithmetical puzzles attributed to the 'Circumlocution Office', and conveys no real idea of the facts. For our Line officer there are neither Sundays nor holidays, and the night brings no remission from labour during the whole year. The whole body of officers have averaged, for each officer for each

day of the year, 1.041 excursions, and 9.268 miles of
regular patrolling (two-thirds of this during the
night), beside the weighment of 194.517 maunds of
goods, office-works, reports, returns, registers, the
preparation of cases, collection of statistics, etc. for the
men, there are six hours of duty by day and six hours
by night, and hedge work off the Line, and lying in
wait on information received, etc., etc., over and above
this. Men and officers are now adequately remunerated,
and complaints are rarely heard, but, for all that, I
believe that under the present system of administration
there is no large body of men in the world from whom
so much unintermittingly and *hard* labour is required.

A Customs Line officer was responsible for a 'beat' of from
ten to thirty miles. He had to be capable of 'great bodily
activity, incessant locomotion, indifference to sun, wind,
weather, and his night's rest'. The only other officers he would
normally meet were the two who ran the adjacent beats. He
might get a visit from his Collector, or the Commissioner
himself or his deputy, perhaps three times in a year. Usually
he was miles from any town. In charge of about a hundred
men, he was expected to keep tight discipline, and not to
fraternise too much with subordinates or the nearby villagers.
Nearly all the officers were British. There was some attempt
to attract Indians, but without much success. With the quali-
fications that were needed, especially the ability to compile
reports in English, likely candidates could find less physically

demanding and better paid jobs elsewhere. A. O. Hume was unconcerned:

> Amongst Europeans, on the contrary (young men fond of sport), this restless laborious life has a charm. Numbers, it is true, enter the department, to leave before their term of probation expires, but of those who remain, the vast majority do this perpetual knocking about at all hours, and in all weathers, more or less *con amore*. They can do their patrolling work as well, if not better, gun in hand; the excitement of the sport, relieves the constant out-door life of much of its unpleasantness, and they live, on the whole, happy, healthy lives, doing good service to the State.

The subordinate men of the Inland Customs Department were recruited from areas other than where they were stationed. Like an army of occupation they could hardly have been popular. In areas where wood was scarce, the huge amounts of brushwood needed for the dry hedge led to major disputes. To minimise friction, villagers close to the Customs Line were allowed to take up to two pounds of salt across duty-free. Nevertheless, they would often have been searched as they crossed the line. This gave plenty of scope for extracting bribes.

It must also be remembered that the Customs Line was not only built to control the passage of salt going into British India, but also to impose a levy on sugar going out. About ten per cent of the revenue collected was from sugar export. This meant that traffic was checked and impeded in both directions. Villagers on both sides of the line had cause for dissatisfaction. On the other hand, the customs men had ready money to spend. Supplying food, drink and other services would have been profitable.

Until 1868 the customs men had to live alone on the Line, without their wives and families.

> The idea was that the men would get quarrelling about the women, would meddle with each other's wives, and would always be with their families instead of out on the Line. Further, it was supposed that the men's wives would make friends with the village women, and through such intimacy be led to seduce their husbands into conniving with smugglers.

However, as Hume further reported:

> As a matter of fact it is running after women that chiefly induces our men to stray from the Line, and it is meddling with women that primarily leads to almost all the quarrels they have with the villagers. A considerable number of men are always more or less unfit for duty owing to venereal diseases. A man with his wife on the Line escapes all these dangers; when, after six hours duty on guard, and four or five of hard hedge-work, he comes back to his hut, to find his food ready cooked; his chil-

dren help him with the hedge; he cannot disappear at a moment's notice; his pay goes further when his family is with him by at least a rupee a month; he is no longer always wanting to get leave to go away and look after his people; his home is on the Line; and dismissal becomes a penalty very greatly dreaded.

Accordingly, as an experiment, some customs men were allowed to live with their wives. Things did not quite work out as anticipated. Many of the Muslims, who constituted a disproportionate 42 per cent of the workforce, took extra 'Line-wives, whose antecedents in a number of cases are anything but respectable.' However, the authorities decided to ignore these difficulties, and the experiment was judged a success. Some other liaisons were severely dealt with. Two men convicted of 'unnatural crimes' were each sentenced to five years in prison.

Housing was not provided: 'In many beats where the live hedge is thriving, wood in abundance is available; while, wherever the hedge is complete and needs comparatively little labour, the men can easily make for themselves the necessary mud walls and a flat mud roof.'

The workforce seems to have reached its peak in 1872, when it totalled 14,188. Afterwards, there was a slight reduction as the hedge generally became more formidable, for the green hedge required less labour than the dry one. Moving the Customs Line to the Agra Canal allowed another reduction in the establishment. In the final year of the line, reduced maintenance allowed a further reduction. However, even at the very end, there was still a total staff of over 10,000.

As with any such large body of men, there was continual wastage. W. S. Halsey, in one of his tables for 1876–7, catalogued the 'casualties' for each grade. In total, 115 men had died, 276 had been dismissed, 30 had deserted when on duty, 360 had failed to rejoin after leave, and 23 were 'removed as unfit'. However, all in all, it was a desirable job. The pay of 5 rupees a month, when compared with the local agricultural wage of about 3 rupees, was relatively high. The men were often stationed in remote areas, where there was the opportunity to save money. There were other opportunities to make money too, since all the proceeds of seized salt went to the captors.

The function of the Customs Line was to deter smuggling. Smugglers and smuggling featured large in all the official reports. There were many complaints that those caught were too leniently dealt with by the magistrates. Commissioner Hume wrote in 1868 – a year when 924 smugglers had paid fines, and 1,416 had been sent to prison:

The mass of the Line smugglers are men more or less

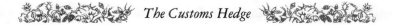

connected with the criminal classes; have no sort of objection to a month's visit to old friends in jail, and infinitely prefer accepting a month's food gratis and keeping their Rs 6 to spend on women and liquor, when they come out of jail, to avoiding this imprisonment, at the expense of the Rs 6 and all it will procure for them. If ever there was a class of offenders, for whom *no* 'just sympathy' could be reasonably felt, it is that which comprises professional smugglers of the Delhi, Agra, and Saugor Divisions.

Since the average fine was over 8 rupees, at a time when the agricultural wage was 3 rupees a month, these remarks seem harsh. However, he went on: 'I do most earnestly advocate the utmost severity the law permits of − a fine, heavy enough to make it difficult to pay, and in default, 6 months' rigorous imprisonment.'

It has to be remembered, too, that there were many other arrests for breaking the salt laws in the Bengal Presidency, other than those on the Customs Line. A completely independent force of customs officers enforced the law in the salt-producing areas. In 1869–70, in the 'Saliferous Districts of the Lower Provinces of Bengal' alone, there were 1,818 convictions. There were large numbers of convictions and imprisonments in both the Bombay and Madras Presidencies. Every year, across the whole of British India, many thousands were imprisoned.

Over the years the number of arrests increased. In years

when the crops failed, when people would have found it particularly onerous to pay the Salt Tax, no allowance was made for hardship. It was still levied from the starving; smuggling was still ruthlessly punished. In the penultimate year of the line, 1877–8, when the Commissioner wrote of 'the distress arising from the high price of grain', 6,077 persons were convicted of smuggling. Of these, 3,252 failed to pay the fine and so were sent to prison for an average of six weeks.

In the early days of the Customs Line, when it was scantily patrolled, large-scale smuggling was common. Armed gangs, with herds of salt-laden cattle, or strings of camels, broke through weakly guarded sections. Even towards the end, there were occasional seizures and confiscation of animals carrying salt. Usually, however, these were not blatant attempts to breach the line, but attempts to disguise goods passing through the checkpoints. A favourite, albeit unlikely, ruse was to pass off salt as dried fruit. Another ploy was to float salt-laden rafts down the rivers at night. The crewless rafts would then be collected many miles downstream.

In areas where the hedge was impossible to force:

A strong sapling, with lateral branches chopped off some few inches from the stem, is rested in a dark night against the hedge; and up this, as up a ladder, the smuggler climbs – the pole, as he mounts, pressing further and further in at the thin top of the hedge, so that at the top he may chance to be able to jump clear on the other side, of course leading to a tell-tale pole behind him . . .

A stout pole is furnished at top with four curved prongs, forming, as it were, the skeleton of a rather deep cup, in which a bag of salt is placed, and, by a jerk of the pole, sent flying over the hedge, to be picked up in due course by some accomplice waiting on the other side.

A more sophisticated ruse was tried, and then blocked:

Namely, that of hiding a quantity of salt within Customs jurisdiction, but above line, and then giving information to the Customs Officers, as if of accidental discovery. Under standing rules the salt is sold and half the proceeds given to the informer without deduction of Government duty. As the salt is sold at a price above Rs 3 the maund, the informer gets more than Rs 1-8-0 [1½ ruppees] per maund, which far exceeds the cost of salt above line.

The main concern, however, was 'head-load' smuggling of loads of a hundred or so pounds of salt:

One or two men, or perhaps a small party, all on foot, and, most of them, each with a bag of salt on his head, attempt during dark nights to cross the line unobserved. Once seen, it was easy for the Customs Officer to catch a smuggler so long as he stuck to his load, but in many parts of the country where salt is very cheap just outside the line, it paid a smuggler well if he succeeded in running one out of every six loads; it was therefore in his interest when discovered to drop his load at once, and equally our interest to capture *him* rather than his *load*, whereby he only lost perhaps one-eighth of what he would gain by the first load he succeeded in passing. To capture the smuggler as well as secure his load, over rough ground, in a dark night, requires great vigilance, a stealthy advance, and much activity and pluck, as many of the smugglers always carry handfuls of sharp stones or ragged kunkur, which they dash suddenly in the faces of their pursuers, when these are about to clutch them.

Head-load smuggling was widespread and risky. Some 6,765 head-loads of salt were seized in 1873–4, and 3,271 of the smugglers arrested. Nor were the smugglers all the low men usually depicted. In Raipur, it was noted, the smugglers were 'men and women of all classes'.

Between the customs men and smugglers violence was common. Every Annual Report dealt with fights, and some-times with loss of life. In 1877–8 for example, during 'the distress caused by the high price of grain':

An opportunity was seldom missed of fighting our men if there was a fair chance of success. In the Hattin beat one case occurred in September, 1877, in which two peons lost their lives in an encounter with 112 smug-glers, who all made good their escape at the time, but were subsequently followed up, and more than half of them secured. Two of the number were sentenced by the criminal court at Gurgaon to transportation for life, and the rest to various terms of imprisonment. In the Sauridad and Kalanaur beats, too, encounters with smugglers came to be at one time of frequent occurrence, and wounds received on both sides a common event. In one of these affrays in Kalanaur a smuggler was so severely handled as to die while awaiting trial; in some instances our men behaved so well as to receive special awards for their bravery . . .

In the Sohar beat, a party of seven Customs men patrolling above the line encountered a gang of, it is estimated, at least 30 smugglers. In his efforts to come up with and arrest the smugglers, one peon, Gomeh Khan, a Rangar more plucky than the rest, got in advance and was killed fighting against great odds. Fourteen of the offenders were caught, some at the time and some afterwards, and brought to justice, and one man was transported for life, one was imprisoned for 10 years, and 12 were imprisoned for 2 years each.

In 1871–2, where 'there was some increase in smuggling owing to the failure of rain in the Sirsa District, which reduced the people to extreme want . . . one smuggler lost his life, it is said from the injuries inflicted by the clubs of his own friends, while he was grappling with the Customs peon who had seized him.' And 'one smuggler was drowned, having jumped into a tank in trying to escape.' The smugglers often had the sympathy of the population at large, but this was stamped on. In 1874–5 'where an entire village turned out to rescue the smugglers, the ringleaders were identified and heavily punished.'

I found the Annual Reports sad reading. There was much fascinating information about the Customs Line and the Customs Hedge. It was an amazing achievement to have grown such a hedge across the sub-continent. The officers and men had shown extraordinary resourcefulness and devotion. Nevertheless, what remained in the mind were the desperate attempts to secure salt of those made destitute by famine.

SEVEN

Salt

*The maintenance of fixed sentries by day and night over
every patch of saline salt in the country is a financial
impossibility. The general rule should be to depend on
frequent inspection of swamps and salt-earth tracts by
parties, whose duty it will be to destroy all small
formations of salt; to report all larger ones to the
Inspector of the range . . . with a view to the employment
of labour for their destruction; and carefully to note all
signs of the removal of spontaneous salt, or the scraping
of salt-earth.*

MANUAL FOR THE GUIDANCE OF OFFICERS OF THE EXCISE AND
SALT DEPARTMENT, Bengal

A s I researched the history of the Customs Hedge, I had
become more and more concerned about the justness of
the Salt Tax. All taxes, of course, are unpopular, but taxes that
bear heavily on the poor are particularly repugnant. If a tax
had been so high that it deprived the poor of an absolute
necessity of life then it would be indefensible. Once again I
was struck by how little information there was in the history

books. There seemed to be nothing about the effect of the Salt Tax on the health of the people.

There was, of course, no doubt that the Indians liked salt. In common with the rest of humanity, they found that it enhanced the flavour of food. Much the same, however, could be said about sugar, which is now generally regarded as an unnecessary luxury. In order to formulate a view on the Salt Tax, I needed to know more about salt.

In recent years there has been much publicity as to the evils of excess salt. Books on health and diet are full of advice on how to reduce consumption. Nowhere is any concern expressed as to lack of sufficient salt. This has so influenced public opinion that many people believe that adding salt to food is entirely unnecessary. Friends of mine were quick to suggest that salt was either not needed by the body, or that there was already sufficient in fruit and vegetables. They then went on to ridicule my qualms about the justness of the Salt Tax. Some even suggested that the British had done the Indians a favour by restricting salt consumption.

It was difficult to discover the truth. From books on human physiology I soon established that salt is, indeed, necessary. Finding exactly how much salt is needed proved much more difficult. Modern processed and cooked foods usually contain salt, since it is cheap and makes them tastier and more saleable. Bread, cereals, butter, margarine, yoghurt, tinned vegetables, jams, biscuits and cakes, all have large quantities of added salt. Similarly, food cooked at home or in restaurants contains plenty of salt. Since salt in this quantity is believed to be harmful, books emphasise the need to reduce consumption, but fail to specify what is the minimum requirement. With the large surplus of salt in most modern diets, it is unlikely that anyone will have salt deficiency. For this reason, there is little literature on minimum salt requirement. After much fruitless searching, I tracked down a book that explored the issue in massive detail, Derek Denton's *The Hunger for Salt: An Anthropological, Physiological and Medical Analysis.* From this vast tome – the product of thirty years' research – and the copious sources it cited, I was able to uncover the scientific facts.

The body needs salt – sodium chloride – to function, for it is a vital constituent of blood and other fluids. It represents about a four-hundredth of body weight. The average human body contains about six ounces of salt. The concentration of salt is critical, and the body will gain or lose water to keep it constant. Human body temperature is kept down by the cooling action of evaporated sweat. When the air is hot, more sweat is generated. Similarly, physical work, which would heat the body, results in more sweating. In a hot climate, especially when hard manual work is being done, considerable quantities of sweat are exuded. During a really hot day this can be two pints an hour.

Sweat contains salt. In hot climates the loss of salt in sweat may exceed an ounce a day. This is about one-sixth of the total in the body. In extreme desert conditions, similar to those in Rajasthan, losses of over three times as much can occur. Half the body's salt can be lost in a single day. In hot dry weather it is sometimes possible to see the salt efflorescence left behind on the skin by the evaporated sweat – the so-called 'salt frost'. To keep the salt concentration in the blood constant, the body will not retain all the water drunk to replenish that lost in sweating. Surplus water will be passed out as urine. The volume of blood in the body will drop. Blood pressure will fall. If the loss of salt continues, the contraction of blood volume will too, and blood pressure will relentlessly fall. The brain will be starved of blood. Fainting, and ultimately total unconsciousness, will result. Before the advent of intravenous drip-feeding, it was impossible to feed unconscious people, so they died.

In modern developed societies there is plenty of salt in the diet. Extra-added salt, although it may be pleasurable, is not usually necessary. Often it is passed out in the urine, and no harm results. However, if the kidneys are overloaded or inefficient, then the body will retain water so as to keep the ratio of salt in the blood constant. Then, the volume of blood will increase, and blood pressure will rise. To keep their blood pressure down, such people should reduce their intake of salt, for high blood pressure has numerous harmful side effects. It puts a strain on the heart muscle, and eventually the heart may fail. It also causes hardening of the arteries, which leads to kidney disease, strokes and coronary artery disease.

The scenario in India in the eighteenth and nineteenth centuries was totally different. Most Indians had no pre-added salt in their diet. The vast majority of the population lived in the countryside. Most food was either home-grown or purchased unprocessed. Even if food were purchased with salt already in, it would, of course, still have had to be paid for. As it was, the villagers baked bread, cooked rice and fried vegetables at home. To all these they added salt.

Human beings crave salt and try to take more than they strictly need – food is more pleasant that way. The evolution of this craving is imperfectly understood, but it may be that it was developed so that high priority was given to seeking out this essential mineral. Like other people, the Indians, if they could afford it, probably added more salt than was absolutely necessary. However, even the poorest Indians added salt if they could. They believed that their health depended on it.

It is also important to take salt regularly. A surplus of salt at one time cannot compensate for a shortage later on. The body cannot store salt for more than a few days. Any excess salt is passed out – mostly in the urine – to maintain the correct concentration in the blood. Consequently the effects of salt deprivation, as the body loses water, will be felt quickly. Volunteers put on a very low salt diet, in temperate conditions, lost over two pounds in the first five days. In tropical climates, hard work produces copious sweating, and more dramatic results. D. B. Dill of the Harvard University Fatigue Laboratory, while drinking plenty of water but taking no salt in a hot environment, lost over four pounds' weight in two days.

Heat exhaustion can be either the result of too little water, or of too little salt. The body's reaction to these states is entirely different. Lack of water produces a thirst, and normally the person drinks, and recovers. Salt depletion, on the other hand, does not produce a thirst, or an enhanced craving for salt. The victim feels unwell but has no idea why. Lassitude, apathy, headaches and muscular weakness are the initial symptoms. More salt depletion may lead to giddiness and fainting. Further depletion will induce anorexia, nausea and vomiting. This will reduce the intake of food, and any salt in it, and lead to further vomiting and salt depletion.

Death from salt depletion, especially when accompanied by another illness, would have often been mis-diagnosed. In the villages it would have been put down to other causes. Even in twentieth-century hospitals, as Dr Marriot has observed: 'Their deaths are ascribed to "toxaemia" or "uraemia" or "circulatory failure" when they have, in fact, died from simple lack of salt, and could easily have been saved.'

Exactly how much salt people require varies. Large bodies need more than small ones. Some people have a more efficient metabolism than others, and may need relatively little salt. Manual workers require more salt than those in sedentary jobs. Some climates, or work environments, are hotter than others, and demand a greater salt intake. It seems that no one has done an exhaustive analysis of the average minimum salt requirement of people in India. In practice, this would be almost impossible to do. A sample of people willing to undergo salt deprivation, and large enough to give a meaningful result, would be difficult to assemble. It would be expensive and probably unethical. Most of all, as salt is now relatively cheap, it would serve no purpose. Moreover, an average figure would be of little use in determining minimum salt requirement. As salt hunger is not linked to salt deprivation, the only way to isolate those who require more than the average intake is to conduct sophisticated medical tests on everyone. This is not possible on a large scale, even now. In the nineteenth century the only safe way to ensure everyone received sufficient salt would have been to pitch consumption to the level of those requiring the most salt.

During the Second World War a number of studies were made on military personnel in tropical climates. Some were British, and some Indian. Some had already fallen ill with the heat, and some were 'volunteers'. These studies showed that even the special tropical allowance of one ounce of salt a day was not always sufficient. A distinguished British consultant physician, Dr H. L. Marriott of the Middlesex Hospital, was seconded to the army in India. He later wrote the classic medical book, *Water and Salt Depletion.* It so happened that he was able to observe the effects of salt depletion inside the area formerly enclosed by the Customs Line:

It was my duty in India to do special tours in the hottest

weather (June) to observe heat effects in such particularly hot stations as Allahabad, Cawnpore, Lucknow,
and Bareilly. The tour of 1942 was particularly instruc-
tive, because it happened to be an unusually hot season
(maximum shade temperatures in the above stations
were between 115° and 123° F [46° and 50.6° C] and
sun temperatures very much higher) and because in that
year – the first real war year for India – there was not
adequate shade provision for men, nor was there general
realisation of the importance of extra salt intake. During
this hot season there were 1,959 admissions to hospital
for heat effects and 136 deaths. I personally saw 400
cases. During my period in the Tropics I also saw salt
depletion complicating the picture in many illnesses –
for example, scrub typhus.

This was despite the high salt content – an ounce a day – of
military food. An ounce of salt a day adds up to 23 pounds a
year. Of course, for some the allowance was adequate, and also
in the cooler season less salt was needed. Taking these factors
into account, it seems reasonable to assume that an average of
at least 12 pounds a year was necessary. Some people may well
have required more, especially if ill. In areas of nineteenth-
century India where salt was relatively cheap, consumption
was about 16 pounds a head. In the Bengal Presidency –
inside the Customs Line – the figures for consumption were a
matter of contention. At the House of Commons enquiry in
1836, the Company, anxious to prove that salt was not exces-

sively taxed, insisted it was about 12 pounds. Other, more independent, witnesses put it at less than eight.

The lower figure was probably more reliable. Some years later, in 1869, the Commissioner of Inland Customs had much more accurate census and other statistics at his disposal. In his Annual Report he wrote:

> Excluding the salt-sources and their immediate vicinity, the average consumption of adults in the belt of country extending for 100 miles outside our cordon, where untaxed salt is available, is certainly not less than 13 lbs. per adult and probably materially exceeds this amount . . . both by actual enquiry and by reference to population and supplies, it is proved that the average consumed by adults within the Line cannot exceed 8 lbs.

It must be emphasised, moreover, that these are average figures. While eight pounds of salt a year for an adult was probably insufficient, many of the poor would have been unable to purchase even that. The lower castes would have been disproportionately affected. Moreover, the British made no tax concessions in years of famine or disease – years when many would have had no cash to buy salt.

Furthermore, India had no long history of salt shortage. In parts of the world where salt is in very short supply, people have adapted their metabolism to those conditions, and tend to lose less salt in their sweat and urine. They have also learnt to avoid waste of what salt they have access to. In India, people were not used to salt being especially precious, and they were not brought up to conserve it. Hence, salt was often wasted – for example, in the discarded water used to boil rice or vegetables. The amount actually consumed would have been considerably less than that used in cooking. Also, since the desire for salt does not increase when the body is deprived of it, they would have tended to use it evenly throughout the year. That was wasteful, since the body cannot store salt. It would have been better to consume less in the cooler season, and more in the sweat-inducing heat. As it was, even those able to afford a theoretically adequate minimum annual intake would have suffered in hot weather.

During the nineteenth century, there were several parliamentary enquiries into salt supply and taxation in British India. These were initiated by those keen to export more British salt to India, and also by those concerned about salt deprivation. British doctors, with wide experience of rural Bengal, gave evidence. They testified that, because of the high tax, many of the population were getting insufficient salt. They asserted that, because of the lack of salt, people had lost their resistance to cholera and to other diseases.

Modern research partly supports this view. Diarrhoea results in a high loss of salt. An ounce or more of salt can easily be lost in a single day. As this is about one-sixth of the body's total, losses of this magnitude soon lead to severe dehydration and death. The principal ingredient of present-day medicines for rehydration is salt. Some Indians thought that cholera was actually caused by the lack of salt. This was not true. Cholera comes from drinking infected water. Continuing to drink such water would probably have led to death in any event. However, where clean water was later available, people without salt would have succumbed nevertheless, because it would have been impossible to rehydrate their bodies.

India also had many other diarrhoea-producing diseases. Indeed, it was notorious for the variety and virulence of its diarrhoeas. Typhus, giardia, and amoebic dysentery were rampant. Children were particularly prone to these and other such infections. The dehydration and salt loss that followed diarrhoea would often have resulted in death. Many other Indian diseases, for example malaria, caused fever and sweating. The salt lost in the sweat had to be replaced, otherwise dehydration occurred. Similarly, vomit also contained large amounts of salt. Thus, being sick led to severe salt depletion, and consequent dehydration. Dehydration severely reduces the body's ability to fight disease, and often culminates in death.

Human milk contains salt. This is lucky for breast-fed children, for at least they receive a modicum of salt in their diet. In a salt-deficient diet, however, the mother suffers, for her own salt reservoir is depleted. Her health is affected, and ultimately this can reduce her milk yield, and the health of her infant. Vomiting, as we have seen, is also a cause of salt loss. Pregnant women, who had problems with repeated vomiting, needed extra salt to avoid dehydration. Apart from the damage to their own health, this would have also induced miscarriages and abnormal births.

In the debates on the Salt Tax, there were conflicting views as to whether farm animals needed salt and whether the Indian farmer gave it. The government made no allowance for its provision. Carnivorous animals do not require extra salt. They get sufficient from the meat of other animals. Humans can get some of the salt they need from eating meat, but need an undiluted meat diet to receive their entire requirement. Most Indians are vegetarian, so this supplement is not an option for them. In any event, most meat eaten by the non-vegetarians comes from cattle, sheep and goats. These herbivores, just like humans, need salt to survive. In some areas of India there is low-grade salt in the soil, which animals can lick. This led some British administrators to assert that extra salt for farm animals was never given, and was unnecessary. This may have been true in some areas, but it was not true in many others. The cow, on which the majority of Indians relied for milk and fuel, needed salt. Lack of salt led to a noticeable decline in cattle health and milk yields.

Contrary to what many believe, fruit and vegetables do not usually contain any appreciable quantity of salt. Since most soils and water sources have no sodium content, and there is no sodium in the air, there is nowhere from where it could come. Near the sea, a minute quantity of salt may be present in rain. Even if the mineral is present in the soil, the quantity taken up into the plant is almost insignificant in relation to what is needed by humans. It has been calculated that, to get enough salt, you would have to eat more than your body weight of fruit and vegetables every day.

One of the consequences of the high tax on salt was that it was often adulterated. People desperate to get salt at an affordable price ended up spending their money on salt that had been heavily diluted with other substances – some harmless, and some noxious. As an 1852 petition from Calcutta put it:

Many proofs that the duty presses with very great severity might be given, but one must here be sufficient, namely, that out of Calcutta, as far as the North-west Provinces, pure salt, as sold by the Government or imported, is almost unknown to the mass of the people; adulterations of all kinds are resorted to reduce its price to their means of purchasing; a wholesome condiment is thus often rendered unwholesome, and as to all purposes for which pure salt is necessary the duty is a prohibition.

It is probable that the depressed salt consumption, which resulted from the Salt Tax inside the Customs Line, had a general effect on the population. Unfortunately, since salt deprivation did not produce an increased craving for salt, even the victims would often not have realised the danger they were in. In times of famine the effects would usually have been ascribed to hunger. At the very least, the poorer sections of the population would have been affected by the lassitude induced by mild salt depletion. This would have affected their work output and food production. They would already have been made poorer by paying the punitively high Salt Tax on

even their reduced intake. The effect upon the ill and the pregnant would have been more severe.

It is, of course, impossible to say how many people were made ill as a result of salt deprivation. We have no idea of how many died. Their deaths were hidden in the copious statistics of deaths from other causes; buried in the mass of deaths reportedly caused by disease or famine. We do know that the government realised that salt consumption was severely reduced by the Salt Tax. We know that even the government's own figures show a consumption way below the minimum considered necessary for their own soldiers in India, and well below the minimum prescribed for prisoners in English jails. We also know that British doctors working in India protested to parliament, and that for the sake of keeping an easily collectable tax the British government ignored them.

It could just possibly be argued that the Salt Tax as it stood towards the end of British rule, although it bore unequally on the poor, was set at a reasonable level. Similarly, the Salt Tax imposed by the British in the territories outside Bengal in the early days could perhaps be justified. However, the level of the Salt Tax inside the Customs Line was totally inhumane.

In order to try to understand the logic behind the construction of the Customs Line, it is necessary to consider the natural availability of salt in India. A barrier could only be effective if it could deprive the population of untaxed salt. Nowadays, salt is such a common commodity, so easily available, that it is easy to assume it occurs naturally throughout the country. In fact, vast tracts of India have no salt. Huge populations live hundreds of miles from the nearest source of salt. India as a whole, however, always had more than sufficient resources for the supply of salt to its population. There were huge deposits of rock salt in the Punjab, and great salt lakes in central India. In addition, the country was surrounded on three sides by sea, from which salt could be extracted. In some areas there were saline wells or salty earth. From time immemorial salt from one or other of these sources had reached all the inhabitants of India. It was only when the British began to administer the country in the late eighteenth century that a huge Salt Tax, together with the barriers necessary to collect that tax, resulted in the population being deprived of salt.

In the Punjab long ranges of hills contained inexhaustible supplies of rock salt. Reserves were estimated at 70,000 million tons. The salt was unusually pure, with only about two per cent impurities, and was often found as huge crystals. The salt lay in outcrops, or in deep strata just below the surface. Some of the mines were among the oldest in the world. Huge caverns had been dug, as much as 250 feet long and 200 feet high. It required minimal effort to extract the salt. Being pure, it only required digging out and breaking up. It was therefore extremely cheap.

The salt lakes, especially Lake Sambhar near Ajmer, also produced huge quantities of salt. This was either left behind, as the lakes contracted in the dry season, or evaporated off by the sun in special enclosures. Either way it was inexpensive to produce. Cheap salt was also produced on the east coast – in Gujarat and near Bombay – by solar evaporation from the sea. Salt was similarly produced at Madras, and other places in south India. There was sufficient salt for the population in those areas, and for some extra to be available to export into the Bengal Presidency.

Nevertheless, because it was difficult to transport salt across a sub-continent that had virtually no roads, a major source of salt for Bengal had always been the eastern sea. To produce salt from that sea, however, was no easy matter. For much of the year, the water discharged by the Ganges and other rivers heavily diluted the sea. In addition, the atmosphere was extremely humid, so as to inhibit solar evaporation. To over-come these problems a complicated and hugely labour-inten-sive industry had developed.

In the Calcutta area, six months of heavy rain came to an end in November. By January, the rivers were low, and it was possible for the salt manufacturers, the *malangis,* and their men, to dam some of the smaller rivers. This meant that the salt-water, being carried up the larger rivers by the spring tides, was kept at maximum concentration. It was then diverted along specially dug canals into salt-water reservoirs.

Around these reservoirs were salt pans – cleared and flattened earth fields, enclosed by mud walls. These pans were flooded with the salt-water, which was then allowed to evaporate. This might be done several times. The earth became rich with salt. The salt-dirt was then scraped up, and taken to a *maidah,* a cone of baked mud with the top scooped out. Salt-water was trickled over the salt-dirt, and the concentrated saline liquor led away to be boiled. In the boiling houses there was an extraordinary arrangement of small earthenware pots, piled in a pyramid over a huge wood-fired stove. The salt-liquor was ladled into these, and then topped up as it evaporated. Eventually, the deposited salt was spooned out.

All this effort needed a vast workforce. Thousands of workers were employed to construct the dams, dig the canals, build the salt pans, extract the salt and, above all, to collect fuel for the boiling houses. At the start of the Company's rule, there were at least 60,000 men employed. The work was hard and notoriously badly paid. A labourer received only 13 *gundas* a day. The *gunda* was a tiny unit of currency, equivalent to only four cowrie shells. There were 100 *gundas* to the *anna*, and 16 *annas* to the rupee. Thus, in a month of thirty working days, a labourer's remuneration would have added up to only a quarter of a rupee.

At the beginning of the Company's rule, those 60,000 workers were producing over 3,000,000 *maunds* of salt a year. The Company was making annual profits of millions of rupees. However, the salt was only sufficient for about a quarter of the population of Bengal. Good sites for salt production were hard to find, and fuel was scarce. Salt was always needed from elsewhere.

Orthodox Hindus were reluctant to use the normally produced salt from the Bay of Bengal. They divided foodstuffs into *kaccha* or *pucca*. *Pucca* foods were cooked in oil, normally clarified butter, *ghee*. They could be cooked outside the home, and in the company of those of lower caste. *Kaccha* foods, by contrast, were cooked in water. These foods, such as rice or lentils, could only be prepared in the sanctity of the home kitchen. Because most Bengali salt was produced by evaporating seawater in boiling houses, it was considered to be *kaccha,* and forbidden. The strict Hindus, therefore, used rock salt, or salt produced by solar evaporation. Both sorts usually had to come from afar and were, of course, more expensive.

The Salt Tax was levied equally on salt of different quality. It gradually became apparent that high-quality English salt from Cheshire and Worcestershire could be shipped out as ballast from Liverpool, at a nominal freight cost, and sold at a profit. The import duty was calculated so as to enable it to be sold at the same wholesale price as locally manufactured salt. The extraordinary result was that by 1850 nearly half the salt consumed in Bengal came from England. The growth of the Indian railways facilitated the influx of cheaply produced salt from elsewhere in India too. Salt manufacture in Bengal – a government monopoly – gradually declined. By 1862 all legal production had ceased. The salt workers, the hereditary *malangis* and their labourers, who had produced Bengal's salt for thousands of years, became landless labourers. When famine struck in 1866 they were among the first to suffer. As Sir Cecil Beadon, Secretary to the Board of Revenue, put it to a Parliamentary Select Committee: 'I am afraid a considerable number of them were swept off the face of the earth.'

The British left India in 1947, but the salt workers were still exploited. The Bengal salt works remained closed, but salt production continued at the mines in the Punjab, at the salt lakes in Rajasthan, and at the salt pans on the southern and west coasts. Unfortunately for India, the great salt mines of the Punjab were now in Pakistan, and it was relatively expensive to manufacture high-quality salt from the salt lakes of Rajasthan. This led to a huge expansion in salt manufacture from the sea.

The best sites for extracting salt from the oceans were in Gujarat. In the years after India's independence production gradually concentrated there. By 1998, 72 per cent of Indian salt was produced in Gujarat. The labour conditions were among the worst in India. Very few Gujaratis were employed – the wages were too low for those relatively affluent people – and most of the labour was drawn from poorer states, such as Bihar. Whole families laboured at scraping up salt from the evaporation pans, then piling it into mounds for removal. Lack of proper footwear and other protective clothing, as they gathered the damp salt, cracked their skin. The intense glare from the salt ruined their eyes. A family was lucky to make 50 rupees [72 pence] a day. No one knew how many workers there were. In order to escape tax and social security payments, and to avoid the laws on the employment of children, the contractors massively under-declared their workforces. Independent estimates suggested that 20,000 were employed at Kandla alone.

On 9 June 1998 a cyclone hit the Gujarat coast. Huge tidal waves rolled across the salt flats at Kandla. The salt workers' makeshift houses were destroyed. Entire families were swept away. The official death toll was 1,126. Social workers believe that at least 14,000 perished. The price of salt in India went up by seventy-five per cent.

Cheap labour was easy to replace. Production was soon resumed. Six months later, a completely new workforce had been installed, and the price of salt was back to normal. As the Gujarati folk song laments:

Oh, mother, why did you marry me to a salt worker?
He has no sense – if he did he would search for some other work.

For many Bihari labourers, however, there was no other work.

In the eighteenth and nineteenth centuries, as in modern times, large-scale salt production was only feasible at a few sites in India. Huge areas without natural salt often separated these centres. It was this geological accident which made it possible to control the movement of salt across India by constructing a barrier. If there had been pockets of salt dotted across the Indian landscape, there would have been no Customs Line, and no Customs Hedge.

I was deeply shocked by what I discovered about salt. When I first had the idea of finding the remnants of the Customs Hedge, I had imagined the barrier as a piece of British whimsy constructed to collect a minor tax. I had assumed it was merely a flamboyant boundary, perhaps fashioned by administrators with fond memories of English hedgerows. It was a terrible discovery to find that it had been constructed, and ruthlessly policed, so as to totally cut off an affordable supply of an absolute necessity of life. Salt starvation had terrible consequences, but these were always glossed over in the official reports. In 1877–8, for example, the Commissioner reported that 3,252 smugglers had been sent to prison, in a year of 'distress arising from the high price of grain'. It was hardly an adequate description of the horror.

In 1877 the rains in the North-Western Provinces were only a third of normal. From Agra to Allahabad the crops failed. There had been excellent harvests in the preceding years but, aided by the new railways, the surplus had been exported. Not only had these reserves been sent to alleviate famine in southern India, but large quantities had also been sent to Britain. There was panic buying, and the price of grain rocketed. However, even if people had money, there was simply not enough grain in the Provinces. According to official accounts, 1.3 million died. This is now considered to be a serious underestimate.

Reading the official reports, it is striking how many of the deaths were assigned to causes other than plain starvation. Malnutrition reduced resistance to infections that then brought death. The most detailed survey was carried out in sixty-two villages in the districts of Agra, Etah and Mainpuri. Only 12 per cent of deaths were ascribed to 'hunger', but 63 per cent to 'fever' and 'bowel-complaints'. As has been seen, salt depletion is often fatal in those illnesses.

During the famine there was some slight suspension of the land tax. There was much criticism of how inadequate that was. There was, however, no remission of the Salt Tax. In that famine, as in all the others, it was charged in full. Smugglers, and those who scraped up salt-earth, were hunted down. The Customs Hedge was relentlessly patrolled.

The North-Western Provinces famine of 1877–8 was not the only one made worse by the high price of salt inside the Customs Line. Famines had occurred periodically since the imposition of the Salt Tax. There had been another famine in the North-Western Provinces in 1868–9. In the last fifteen years of the Customs Line, there were also famines in Orissa, Bihar, North Bengal and the Central Provinces. For those years only the official reports gave a total of 3,761,420 famine deaths. The real total was probably nearer 5,000,000. People who needed all their money for grain could not afford to buy salt. Very many of the victims died of fever and diarrhoea, and were doubtless speeded on their way by salt depletion.

As I uncovered the truth about salt starvation, I began to think it would be wrong if all signs of this oppression had disappeared, as though it had never happened. Surely, I thought, some remnant of the Customs Line must survive, to keep the memory alive.

EIGHT

A Ridiculous
Obsession

I will but look upon the hedge.

WILLIAM SHAKESPEARE, *The Winter's Tale*

I flew back into Delhi at the beginning of November 1998. I had a month's holiday, and a tight schedule. I had decided that this would be my final attempt to find the Customs Hedge. If I were unsuccessful, I would abandon my search. My friends and colleagues had become bored with my continual talk of the hedge. My brain had room for nothing else. It was becoming a ridiculous obsession. I could not spend the rest of my life chasing a chimera.

First, I wanted to go to Hyderabad to consult with the National Remote Sensing Agency, to see whether they had satellite images that showed the Customs Line. Then, I intended to have a few days' holiday on the Narmada River, at Omkareshwar. There I could acclimatise to the weather, take long walks, and toughen myself up for the serious walking

145

across the Indian countryside that was to come. Over the year since I had last been in India, I had been leading a very sedentary life. My muscles definitely needed some toning. After that, I would meet up with Santosh in Gwalior and go with him to search for the hedge. Where we went would depend on what I found out in Hyderabad.

Over the past year, since my disappointment at Jhansi, I had relentlessly continued my search for more maps. I had not been very successful. I had consulted many experts on Indian history – professors and lecturers, librarians and archivists – but none had even heard of the Customs Hedge. No new large-scale maps had come to light. My only success had been to find a complete set of the fourteen-volume *North-Western Provinces: A Satistical, Descriptive and Historical Account*, in the library of the School of African and Oriental Studies at London University. They were not so tightly bound as the India Office set, and easier to photocopy. I already had a copy of the Jhansi map – the one I had used without success at Khailar. I was able to supplement it with a photocopy of the 1876 map of Etawah District. The scale – eight miles to the inch – was not ideal, but it showed the general location of the Customs Line clearly enough.

During my search for maps, several people had suggested I might use aerial photographs, or satellite images, to find the remnants of the hedge. Aerial photographs did not seem practicable, since there was no publicly accessible archive. Hiring a plane would have been far too expensive and probably prohibited for security reasons. Satellite images seemed more promising. I found that several commercial companies advertised on the Internet. Most of the samples they showed, however, did not reveal sufficient detail. Two or three years in the future they expected to be able to offer much more definition. With what was currently available, I was not sure the Customs Hedge would show up.

India, I had been told, had sophisticated satellite-image technology. It had its own satellites in space, and there was an imaging facility in Hyderabad. I planned to visit there, and find what was available. Fortunately, I was able to book a ticket on the Rajdhani Express in London. This avoided the prospect of queues and waiting at Delhi, which could have easily absorbed three days. As it was, I had a firm reservation to leave the day after I arrived.

In Delhi I stayed with Didi, and caught up on all the gossip. The talk was all of onions – and of salt. Heavy rains and flooding had ruined the vegetable crops. The price of potatoes had doubled. The price of onions had soared from 10 rupees a kilogram to 50. The onion has a special place in the Indian consciousness – Hindu ascetics denounced it as a stimulant, while others extolled its virtues as a food for the poor. There was a belief that, at the very least, a poor man should be entitled to bread and onions. The price of onions was an important issue in politics. At one time Indira Gandhi, campaigning to become Prime Minister, had drawn attention to the then high price of onions by garlanding herself with them. The present government had compounded the problem by continuing to export some of the previous crop, when it was already clear that the current crop would fail. Shortages of essentials, hoarding, and

black-marketeering had become the political issues of the day.

Then, suddenly, just before I arrived, the price of salt had rocketed. Rumours had swept the country that salt supplies were exhausted. Its price in Delhi rose, from 5 rupees a kilogram, to 20. There was panic buying, and the shops were emptied. People were abruptly made aware that they could not live without salt; that this previously mundane condiment was an essential. In other parts of India the panic was worse. In Bihar the price soared to 60 rupees. The police had to break up riots in Patna, Danapur, Arrah, Charia and Dahanabad. Shops were looted across the state.

There was some logic behind the panic. People still had in their minds the cyclone in Gujarat that June, which had killed many of the salt workers. In the fevered atmosphere caused by other shortages, it was easy to imagine salt might have become scarce too. However, the 14,000 or so labourers that had been swept away in Gujarat had already been replaced from India's unlimited reservoirs of poor and unemployed. The salt godowns there had new stocks. Ministers went on television to explain that there was no shortage. They posed inside vast warehouses bulging with salt. The panic ended. The price of salt returned to normal. Nevertheless, the people of India had learnt a lesson as to the value of salt. My friends kept an extra bag in their cupboards – just in case it disappeared again.

The Rajdhani Express lived up to its reputation, and whisked me down in air-conditioned comfort to Hyderabad at speed. In fact, I could have done without the air-conditioning which, as usual, was too cold. However, it was over a thousand miles to Hyderabad, and the Rajdhani got me there in less than a day. The train actually went to Secunderbad, the old British military town, which was a few miles from Hyderabad proper. Sue and Ranjan, friends made on my earlier visit, were waiting at the station. I was looking forward to staying with them, in their stylish modern house set in a lush garden of flowering trees, and also to wandering around old Hyderabad again.

Hyderabad is one of my favourite Indian cities. The old bazaar has a special fascination for me, with all the bustle and interest of Old Delhi, but none of the traffic or pollution. The food is first rate, too. I feasted on aubergines cooked in coconut and tamarind juice; fried bread-pudding sprinkled with almonds. The main purpose of the trip however, was to visit the National Remote Sensing Agency. I had already advised them of my impending arrival, and sent on a description of the Customs Hedge and the co-ordinates of the spots in which I was interested. From Delhi I had telephoned to ask my friends to try and make an appointment for me. That had proved impossible, as the Director was 'out of station'.

In India the whole business of access to maps and land photographs is a nightmare. It is one of the best-mapped countries in the world. The British put huge resources into map-making, and that continued after independence. The

Survey of India produces detailed and up-to-date maps of the entire country. Unfortunately, they are impossible for the general public to obtain. Large-scale maps can only be requisitioned by government departments, and possession by others is illegal. It is also against the law to take any map of a scale larger than 1:250,000 out of the country. This is all in the name of national security. There is much fear about the threat from Pakistan, China and even the CIA. Of course, India does have real concerns over security, but the advent of satellite photography has made such restrictions on maps absurd. When searching the Internet for what was commercially available, I had come across SPOT Imaging Corporation's 'Picture of the month' – a beautifully clear picture of the space launching facilities at Kourou in French Guiana. During the Gulf War the Americans had released extraordinary detailed images of installations in Iraq.

I could have approached one of the various commercial suppliers of satellite images outside India to see if they had what I wanted. However, it had seemed to me that it would be better to start with the government organisation in India, as they were more likely to have what I wanted from stock. With any luck, they would be able to show me images of the hedge areas from their archive. I also thought it would be cheaper. Luckily, the day I arrived in Hyderabad, the Director of the National Remote Sensing Agency, Dr Rao, had returned. There was a wait while I faxed through my references, and passport and visa details, but eventually I was able to make an appointment for the following day.

The Agency was housed a few miles outside Hyderabad, in a complex at Balanagar. After my documents had been thoroughly scrutinised, I was taken to Dr Rao's office. He made me very welcome. Two of his senior colleagues were there and all of them were extremely interested in my project. They had laid out sample photographs to show what they could do.

The detail obtainable on a satellite image is limited by the resolution of the system, the 'resolution' being the smallest object that can be seen. Early systems had a resolution of ten metres; that was, they could show up any object with a diameter of over ten metres. As I knew from my researches on the Internet, there were systems commercially available that had a resolution of three metres. Within a couple of years, it was expected that one-metre resolution images would be available. I had seen mock samples that showed individual people sitting round a swimming pool. Defence departments around the world, of course, had even more resolution at their disposal. Another factor was colour. The earlier and cheaper systems gave images in black and white; the newer and more expensive systems produced them in colour. Foliage shows much better in colour.

'In 2000, we shall have two-metre colour resolution,' Dr Rao said. 'But now we only have five-metre in black and white, and ten-metre in colour.'

'I've been told,' I said, 'that to find the hedge it needs at least five-metre colour resolution, and preferably three-metre.'

'Yes, probably. What we can do though, is overlay the black and white image with the colour. That way, from the merged image, you get almost as good results as from a five-metre colour system. Look at this.'

We went over to a side table where there was a large photograph of Varanasi, the holy city on the bank of the Ganges. The colours had been reversed and enhanced, so that green stood out as red. Little red blocks were probably gardens, and the avenues of Banaras Hindu University were clearly visible. It was quite impressive.

'So you're the experts,' I said. 'What do you think? Will the Customs Hedge show up on one of these?'

'It depends,' said Dr Dutt, an ecologist. 'If there is still a solid line of large trees, it should be visible. The problem might be, if it were the same colour as the surrounding country. Then it would be camouflaged.'

'And how long will it take to produce an image for me? And how much will it cost?'

They told me that it would take a few days to get out an estimate. Once I had given the go-ahead, it might take another two weeks to produce the photographs. I tried to get a rough estimate of the cost, but without success.

I was very disappointed. Previous experiences in India had led me to distrust official predictions of when things might get done. I had a nasty feeling that the 'few days' to produce the estimate might lengthen into weeks; that the 'two weeks' to do the work might turn out to be much longer. I feared that I was most unlikely to get any useful information on my present trip. My hopes of an archive of images being laid out for my inspection had been dashed. I was going to have to search the countryside of Uttar Pradesh without the benefit of space technology. If I failed to find the Customs Line in any of the areas I had pinpointed as likely, and if, nevertheless, the terrain looked promising, I might go ahead later and commission a photograph. Meanwhile, I confirmed the longitude and latitude of the possible site at Erich, and asked them to send me an estimate.

'Come back to us in a couple of years' time, and we'll have two-metre equipment,' Dr Rao said, as I left. 'That should definitely show what you want.' Dr Dutt walked out with me to the car park.

'Good luck,' he said, as we shook hands. 'By the way, in that description of the Customs Hedge you sent, there was a list of all the plants. I've checked them out and I'm afraid none of them lives longer than sixty years. So, unless it has re-seeded, everything might well have disappeared.' He shook his head. 'I do hope not.'

'Thanks,' I said.

That evening I talked things through with Sue and Ranjan. They would try and hurry up the estimate from Balanagar, but were not hopeful. I also had to accept that none of the original trees might be alive. It was not an auspicious start to my trip. I had allowed plenty of time at Hyderabad, imagining myself sifting through countless photographs of the Indian landscape. As it was, I decided to spend a couple of days sightseeing, and then leave for Omkareshwar.

My fears as to how long it would take to receive an estimate from the National Remote Sensing Agency turned out to be fully justified. Over the next month, as I travelled the country, I regularly checked with my friends in Hyderabad as to whether anything had materialised. An estimate finally arrived during my last week in India – too late to pursue. In any case, it was way beyond my means. Just for the one site, at Erich, four overlapping merged photographs were needed. The price quoted was US $16,000.

Omkareshwar is in Madhya Pradesh, forty miles south of Indore. It lies on the Narmada River, one of the holiest in India. The old town is on an island, which is in the shape of the Sanskrit syllable *Om*, written: ॐ. For Hindus, this syllable, and its sound, represents the essence of God. In addition, in the Sri Omkareshwar Mahadeo Temple on the island, there is one of the twelve *Jyotrilinga* – the *lingams* of light – where energy was believed to flow from the earth. Naturally, such a site has been a place of pilgrimage for many centuries. Yet – and I had been there in 1993 – for most of the year there was only a trickle of worshippers. It was another of my favourite places; perfect for me to adjust from my London routine.

It took a laborious series of trains to travel the 650 miles from Hyderabad to Indore, then two bus rides to Omkareshwar. I managed to rent a small house, high on the cliff facing the island. It gave me a wonderful view over the river. I watched the pilgrims below cross the Narmada in flat-bottomed boats, to and from the ghats of the Mahadeo Temple. I watched them feed the sacred fish. At dusk oil-lamps floated down on leaves to prick the river with light. Each night a brown fish-owl settled on my roof and boomed out its cry across the river gorge.

Every day I went for long walks. Being November, the weather was cool in the mornings. I would set off with goose pimples on my arms but by mid-morning I was sweating. It had always been a mystery to me how in parts of India lying so far north of the equator it could sometimes feel so hot in the winter. Most days I followed the old pilgrim path, which made a circular tour – the *parikrama* – of the island, and passed through the holy sites. There were shrines and old ruins everywhere. In the late afternoon I would walk again up to the point of the island, where the sacred streams met. Or I would climb the cliffs to where the devotees of Bhairava, an aspect of Shiva, used to jump off to their death on the rocks below. Parts of the island were high, and there was plenty of climbing to do. The exercise did me good. I began to feel fit.

The food in Omkareshwar was simple. Being a Hindu shrine, it was, of course, a totally vegetarian town. Even eggs were forbidden. The food was the standard of the Hindi-speaking heartland of India – vegetables, lentils, and *chapatis*. It was a diet, once I had adjusted to it, that I found very acceptable. A delicious treat was also available – cream yoghurt, blended with lychees and saffron.

Refreshed and fit, it was almost time for me to meet Santosh at Gwalior. However, as my stay in Hyderabad had been shorter than planned, I had a little time in hand. I diligently studied *Trains at a Glance,* the essential guide for rail travellers. I discovered that I could reach Gwalior in time, even if I travelled from Indore via Delhi and Phulera. Now, Phulera was the stop for Sambhar Lake City, and it was from Lake Sambhar that most of the salt came that had crossed the Customs Line. I knew some salt still came from there. It seemed a good opportunity to see how it was manufactured.

On my last morning in Omkareshwar I went to the Amareshwara Temple. I much preferred it to the Sri Omkareshwar Mahadeo Temple, which was always crowded, and where the priests were grasping. The Amareshwara Temple was over a thousand years old and tranquil. I arrived just before eleven o'clock, in time to see the ceremony in memory of Rani Ahilya Bai. The Rani had been the widowed daughter-in-law of Malhar Rao, the eighteenth-century ruler of Indore. She had been given power over the state – which stretched over much of central India – and was a byword for efficient government, justice and charitable work. Her beautiful profile was still to be seen, framed on the walls of many homes, often garlanded with flowers, or with an oil-lamp burning in front.

At eleven, as on every day since 1795, when the Rani had died, the priests came to sit at the entrance to the temple. There were four of them, each with an antique indented wooden board and a pile of mud from the Narmada. They gestured for me to sit with them. They then began the laborious task of filling each indentation with a little clay *lingam*. Each was then topped with a grain of rice. The priests worked with concentration, chanting prayers, until every indentation was filled, until they had made 1,325 *lingams*. They then sprinkled the *lingams* with water, milk and flower petals. Later, the *lingams* would be cast into the Narmada River, and more mud would be gathered, so as to repeat the ceremony the following day.

I entered the sanctum of the temple and prayed to Lord Shiva. I prayed for success in finding the Customs Hedge. Then, feeling guilty for invoking such a frivolous cause, I prayed for the wellbeing of my family and of my friends.

The train schedule I had worked out was tight, perhaps even optimistic. I had a great admiration for Indian Railways, which managed to transport a huge number of passengers over vast distances at minimal cost. The needs of the poor, unlike on many other rail systems, were given some consideration. Nevertheless, it had to be admitted they were not always on time. The schedule had me arriving at Phulera, from Indore, at mid-day, then leaving on another train for Delhi that same evening. Since the Indore train originated way down south, and could easily have been delayed, I was prepared for the worst.

In fact, the train arrived in Indore at ten o'clock in the evening, exactly on time. I had also managed, against all odds, at such short notice, to secure a reservation in a non-air-conditioned first-class compartment. I had wanted to see the Rajasthan countryside unimpeded by cloudy double-glazing. Delighted, I leapt aboard. One of the merits of the class of travel I had chosen was that the door to the corridor locked. I soon located the compartment shown on my ticket, for there were only three similar ones. I banged hard on the shut door. There was no reply. Further banging caused shouts of anger, then a cautiously opened door. I craned to look inside. All four berths were full. I was protesting that I had a reservation for that compartment, when the door was slammed shut. I hammered on the door with my fist, again and again. There was no response. All was quiet.

I rushed to the carriage door and surveyed the platform, where I spotted a conductor, resplendent in black and gold. He listened to my tale.

'Don't worry,' he said, setting off for the front, air-conditioned, part of the train, 'as soon as we depart, I'll come back and sort things out for you.'

A few minutes later the train pulled out. I lodged my rucksack into a corner of the corridor, sat on it, and waited.

Half an hour passed, with no sign of the conductor. I began to nod off, but forced myself to stay awake. I needed a proper bed if I was to be alert in the morning. Another fifteen minutes passed before I decided to go in search of the conductor. I edged my way through the gloomy corridors of the second-class sleeping compartments, towards the front of the train. After traversing three carriages I abruptly came to a halt. A metal roll-down door barred the way. I shook it hard, but it was securely locked. Dejected, I started to return.

My eyes had become adjusted to the gloom. Looking about me as I negotiated the way back, I surveyed the sleeping forms. I suddenly saw an empty upper bunk. It was difficult to know what to do for the best – should I return to where I had been, and hope for rescue, or should I take the opportunity to bed down and risk being turfed out if the berth was claimed further down the line? There was no one to ask, since everyone was asleep. I was terribly tired. I unrolled my sleeping bag and climbed up.

I soon fell into a deep sleep, from which I was suddenly awoken. The man in the berth below was shouting and cursing. He was kicking out in the direction of the men in the bunks opposite. Since going to sleep, my eyes had become more efficient in the dimness. I looked down under my bed. The man was completely shackled. He was handcuffed and chained, and fastened to the bed-frame.

'What's going on!' I exclaimed, in Hindi.

'I need a piss!' he shouted. 'I need a piss!'

'What do you want me to do?'

'Wake them up.' He pointed with his foot. 'Please, sahib, wake them up!'

Half asleep, I climbed down. I shook one of the sleeping figures. He sprang up, clutching a rifle he had secreted under his blanket. I pointed to the cursing prisoner. The guard mumbled something and made as if to continue sleeping. I shook him again. Reluctantly, he woke up his colleague, and they began the complicated opening of countless locks with double keys. Eventually, the prisoner was able to flee to the toilet. This coincided with our pulling into a station. However, the guards showed no concern that their charge might escape. They turned over and went back to sleep. When the prisoner returned, I had to wake them again, and he meekly offered up his hands to be reshackled.

I had just gone back to sleep, when I was again awoken. This time it was an emissary from the conductor. We were at a station and, if I hurried forward along the platform, an air-conditioned berth had been found for me. I grabbed my bags and ran off at speed.

I arrived at Phulera tired, but on time. It was a small dusty town, with camels in the broad main street. It was good to see cheerful Rajasthanis again, with their brilliantly coloured fabrics and heavy silver jewellery. There was a tea stall beneath a giant banyan tree. I sat there for a while, under its hanging roots, sipping ginger tea, and questioned turbaned and heavily ear-ringed men about local buses. Then, I walked to the other end of the town and, almost immediately, found a bus going the two or three miles to Sambhar.

The grandly named Sambhar Lake City was little more than a village. Transport might have been a problem but, just as I was scanning the empty street, a two-wheeled horse-drawn *tonga* trotted up. I engaged it for a comprehensive tour of 'everywhere and everything'. As we set off, a self-appointed

guide, Donav Ram, asked to join us. As he seemed to have a good knowledge of the area, I took him along.

Sambhar is the largest salt lake in India. In the rainy season it can be twenty miles long, but is often smaller. It is very shallow – on average only two feet deep. It seems to be an inexhaustible source of salt, and has been exploited from time immemorial. No one knows from where the salt came. Some say it was deposited when the region was under the sea; others that it has been blown by the wind from the Rann of Kutch in Gujarat. The most generally accepted theory is that the salt originated locally and has been produced by the decomposition of granite-like rocks deep below. From there the salt has either migrated naturally upwards or, as some believe, moved upwards as brine through a fault in the rocks. The small rivers that flow into the lake drain a huge catchment area, many times the size of the lake itself. Whatever the origin, the salt is fully replenished every year. Originally, salt that was left behind in a thin crust as the lake contracted in the hot dry season was merely scraped up. Later, the process became more sophisticated. The salt water was drained into deep earth pans to evaporate under the sun and thus leave behind a thicker deposit. The British developed this refinement further.

The *tonga* trotted west out of Sambhar Salt City. Soon the lake came into view. As far as the eye could see there were large stone-walled enclosures, the size of cricket pitches, full, or half-full, of murky water. There were other similar enclosures, with semi-dry salt at the bottom. It looked rather grey. Further ahead there was a substantial embankment, running

161

north across the lake, which carried the Jaipur to Jodhpur railway. There was no sign of activity.

'In the British time there were thousands of workers,' Donav Ram said. 'Now there are only a hundred or so. All the business has gone to Gujarat.'

'Why?'

'It must be cheaper to produce the salt there.' He grinned. 'Or maybe someone has been bribed.'

We trotted over the railway embankment, to continue west along the southern shore. More walled enclosures filled the area of the lake. We came to a dam, which ran for a couple of miles straight across to the northern shore, separating the salt pans in the east from the main body of the lake. There were sluice gates through which the lake water was channelled after the monsoon, so that it could be evaporated off in the salt pans. The main lake was attractive. A thin crust of salt ran around the edge, indicating where the water level had dropped by evaporation. There were a number of plovers and ducks. In the shallows there were flocks of flamingos. Some stood far away, in the centre of the lake, showing how shallow much of it was. Here and there were small salt pans where, Donav Ram told me, some salt was still privately made by the villagers.

On the way back we stopped at a beautiful group of temples ringed round a small weed-choked lake. They were semi-derelict, but in their heyday they must have looked very similar to the magnificent white temples and ghats at Pushkar. We went to the railway station, and the nearby factory. The vast buildings were full of heavy machinery, but it was mostly silent. The plant was obviously operating at minimal capacity. The conveyor-belts were still. A few women were building a pile of salt by hand. They carried the salt up on their heads in baskets. I took a photograph, and they waved.

Back at the town we made a tour of the salt company's complex. It was all on a grand scale, with wide avenues of flowering trees, neat rows of workers' cottages, and managers' bungalows set in vast gardens. Although many of the buildings were still in use, there was an air of decay. The gardens were overgrown. We came across a two-storey domed and arched building, still bearing the notice 'Sambhar Salt-Museum'. It was locked and empty. In the grounds outside there was a large model in stone, showing all the salt pans and factory buildings in meticulous detail. It was half-buried in drifted sand.

'It's a pity you didn't come a few years ago,' Donav Ram said, as he drove me back to the bus stand.

'Yes,' I said. 'It is.'

It was all a bit depressing, and a long cry from the bustle of life there under the British. It was even further removed from the days of glory under the Maharajas of Jaipur and Jodhpur, when the salt had supplied much of India, when smugglers had loaded up their camel trains to breach the Customs Line, when the word 'Sambhar' had been a synonym for salt.

I caught the overnight train to Delhi, where I spent the day with friends. Early next morning I took the Shatabdi Express to Gwalior. Three hours later I was there, 200 miles south, shaking hands with Santosh. It was a year since I had seen him, and he was now twenty-three. He looked exactly the same – slim, neat, and still with a boyish manner. However, he was not so cheerful as before. He seemed to have something on his mind; something distracting him.

'Are you feeling all right?' I asked. 'You do want to come with me?'

'Oh, yes,' he said, looking alarmed, 'definitely. I really want to go travelling with you.' He looked me in the eye. 'This time, this time, Royji, we will find the hedge!'

During the day, as his family spoiled me with dishes of aubergine and okra – my favourites – I told Santosh my plans. I spoke of the sites I had identified as hopeful, where the Customs Line appeared not to be buried beneath a road.

'First,' I said, 'we'll go to Jhansi District. From Jhansi town we'll go south to Babina, and afterwards north-east to Erich. If we don't find anything there, then we'll travel up to Etawah District, and search between the Yamuna and Chambal Rivers.'

'Let's hope we find the hedge in Jhansi,' Santosh said, 'the land between the Yamuna and the Chambal is full of bandits!'

Next morning we took a train to Jhansi. We checked into the Jhansi Hotel – where I had stayed two years before. Partially repainted, but with the same battered old paintings and plumbing, it still had a faded Raj ambience. I needed to reset my GPS satellite navigator for local conditions. Since the weather was clear, I decided to do it from Jhansi fort. It was just possible, I thought, that with better visibility than on my trip there two years before, I might see a trace of the Customs Line. Also, I now had a more accurate map with which to align my compass.

When we reached the fort the sky was cloudless. Nevertheless, a pollution pall hung over the city. I was unable to see much further than last time. I lined up the compass with care, but saw nothing. Next morning we took a bus south to Babina. It was the same bus on which I had travelled the previous year to reach Khailar. As we passed through there, I looked west. I saw once again the rough terrain I had searched so painstakingly, so fruitlessly, until I had been stopped by the sound of heavy gunfire. According to the old map, the Customs Line left the main Jhansi to Lalitpur road at Khailar, and then swung back at a right angle to rejoin the main road at Babina. It was a deviation – presumably to follow the old border between Orcha and Jhansi states – of only a dozen miles. From Babina we would be exploring it from the other end.

As we entered Babina my heart sank. There were military personnel everywhere. Huge barracks lined the road into the town; perfectly turned-out non-commissioned officers in camouflage dress strode the streets; black cars full of beribboned officers swept past. There seemed to be nothing left of the old town – the one on my map. Only the ruined stump of a temple on a nearby hill seemed to date from earlier times. All the buildings on the main street looked modern. I was reluctant to draw attention to myself by asking questions. As it was, I felt terribly conspicuous. I was nervous at the thought of being found with maps, compass, and a GPS satellite navigator. Spy mania was still gripping the country. I noticed lots of posters for the ruling Bharatiya Janata Party. They showed the Prime Minister beneath the mushroom of the recently exploded atomic bomb, with the Hindi slogan 'Now India has become great.' I put aside any thought of surreptitiously taking a GPS reading.

Assuming that the main road ran from north to south, we casually strolled down the avenues leading west – towards where the Customs Line should have been. Soon we were in the cantonment area. There were army buildings everywhere. Armed guards stood at the entrances. Fortunately, it was also the way to the railway station, so we had a legitimate destination. We walked down the long avenue. The trees had immaculately painted white trunks. At the end was a square, and the station. If I had not lost my sense of direction, the Customs Line was somewhere on the other side of the tracks. We walked on to the platform to look.

There was a high wire fence on the other side of the station, with army buildings beyond. Suddenly, there came the boom of heavy guns. Wave upon wave of deep sound rolled towards us. The whole landscape was being pounded by artillery. It was probably the firing range I had previously heard from the Khailar side. Santosh and I looked at each other. He shrugged hopelessly, then shook his head. I walked to the booking hall and bought two tickets back to Jhansi.

NINE

Rebellion

*There is no article like salt outside water by taxing which
the State can reach even the starving millions, the sick,
the maimed and the utterly helpless. The tax constitutes
therefore the most inhuman poll tax that ingenuity of
man can devise.*

Mahatma Gandhi

History is full of wars and revolts over salt. Inevitably,
when a scarce commodity is essential for life itself, men
will fight over it. In many places salt is naturally available.
There, normally, it is of little account. In other areas it is not
easily obtainable, and control of supply gives wealth and
power. If salt production is concentrated in a few places
within a country, or if it has to be imported, then it is possible
for rulers to control distribution. Once there is a monopoly, it
is easy for those rulers to impose a Salt Tax.

China has an incredibly long history of salt control. As early
as 2200 BC tribute was being taken as salt. China's long coastline
was not so productive of salt as might be supposed, since the

167

seawater was heavily diluted by the huge outflows of fresh water from the Yangtze and Yellow Rivers. By the third century BC, salt was being extracted by drilling for subterranean brine, pumping it up through bamboo pipes, and then evaporating it in pans heated by burning natural gas. By the seventh century AD, brine was being extracted from as deep as 3,000 feet, with hundreds of wells under the control of the Board of Revenue. Sea salt was also taxed. By AD 900 the Salt Tax was the most important item of government revenue. On China's western border, salt was so scarce that it was used as currency. The salt was made up into small cakes. As Marco Polo observed in the thirteenth century:

> The stamp of the grand khan is impressed, and it cannot be prepared by any other than his own officers. Eighty of these cakes are made to pass for one saggio of gold. But when these are carried by the traders amongst the inhabitants of the mountains and other parts little frequented, they obtain a saggio of gold for sixty, fifty, or even forty of these salt cakes as they find the natives less civilised, further removed from the towns, and more accustomed to remain on the same spot.

Salt continued to be a major source of revenue in China until the seventeenth century, when the administration collapsed. That was not the end of the tax, however, for it was revived in the early twentieth century, under foreign influence, to repay Chinese government loans.

In China, even in the twentieth century, the penalties for flouting the salt laws were severe. For relatively minor offences the punishment was eighty or a hundred blows across the back of the thighs with a heavy flat bamboo stave, together with up to three years banishment; for more serious offences, the beating and 'perpetual exile to some place distant three thousand *li*', one thousand miles, away. It seems, however, that smuggling still occurred on a large scale. As in other countries, though, the lower cost was not passed on to the consumer. The missionary, Joseph Edkins, noted: 'The poor around suffer by this high price of salt; it is one of the elements which increases the dearness of living, and it falls heavily on the poor.'

I spent a whole day in the library of the School of Oriental and African Studies in London, trying to calculate what proportion of a Chinese peasant's wages might have been taken to provide sufficient salt. It was a daunting exercise. Prices of salt, at various times, were expressed in different currencies and weights. *Catty, chin, tan,* and *pical* of weight were costed in *cash, yuan,* or dollars. Incomes were expressed sometimes using these units, and sometimes in the value of bars of silver. In one book I found the advice, 'Unless otherwise indicated the dollar is always the Mexican dollar.' The Mexican dollar! Why was it all so complicated, or was I just stupid? I cheered up when I discovered an entry in *The Encyclopaedia Sinica:*

The taxes existing in 1913 consisted, generally speaking, of a direct tax around which was grouped a most complicated medley of additional taxes imposed from time to

169

time as necessity arose or opportunity offered, and seldom if ever abolished when once imposed.

Levied upon producer, transporting merchant and consumer indiscriminately, collected at any convenient point along the route which the salt had to pass, calculated according to different scales and in various currencies, to five or even eight places of decimals and allocated for such diverse purposes as conservancy, upkeep of schools, the Boxer Indemnity, upkeep of gunboats, support of horse breeding in the Manchu city at Hangchow, of the Association for giving alms to priests, of widows, life-saving institutions and the association for the prevention of killing of animals, they were such as to baffle the most earnest enquirer.

Tempted as I was to abandon my calculations, I persevered. Eventually, I was able very roughly to calculate the relative cost of salt. The price of salt in the nineteenth century seems to have been approximately equal to that of rice. The Chinese Salt Tax did, no doubt, press on the poor who struggled to find enough money just for basic food. Compared to the Salt Tax levied by the British in Bengal, however, it was relatively small. Whereas the Indian peasant had to find two months' wages to pay for his family's yearly salt, most Chinese peasants seem to have lost only about two days' pay.

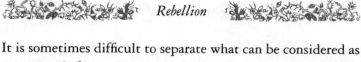

It is sometimes difficult to separate what can be considered as a tax on salt from what is merely the revenue accruing from a salt monopoly. This is particularly true in parts of Africa where salt was scarce. Timbuctoo, for example, was built on the profit from salt coming from Taoudenni. The salt deposits there were in the middle of the Sahara Desert, 400 miles north of Timbuctoo. The merchants of Timbuctoo were able to organise and give armed protection to the huge caravans that brought the salt south. It was a costly and risky enterprise. The caravans were often attacked. Dust storms caused disastrous delays. On several occasions supplies did not get to Taoudenni in time, so everyone died. The mines then had to be restaffed. In 1805 an entire caravan, with 1,800 camels and 2,000 men, died of thirst. If a caravan reached Timbuctoo, however, there were vast profits to be made, selling the salt at the exorbitant price allowed by the monopoly. The merchants were thus able to extort money from a huge area that had no other salt source. Like the salt *malangis* in India, the people who actually extracted the salt received little of this wealth. Until recently the mines were largely staffed by slaves. This continued even under French rule.

In 1974, after Mali had achieved independence, I travelled on a small boat up the River Niger from Mopti to Timbuctoo. A little before Timbuctoo, in open desert, we stopped at the edge of the river and waited. Later that day, a caravan of several hundred camels appeared. The riders wore robes of the deepest indigo, almost black, which glistened with a blue sheen in the brilliant light. The colour had rubbed off, so that even the riders' skins had a blue glow. The men were bringing slabs of salt from Taoudenni – large grey blocks, the shape and size of tombstones, slung in panniers on both sides of the camels. We loaded the boat until we were dangerously low in the water. I spoke, in French, to one of the camel men:

'Do they still use slaves in the mines?'

'No, no,' he protested, 'not now. Of course not. Now, all the work is done by political prisoners.'

It is in Europe, however, that we find the closest parallels with the Salt Tax in India. The Roman state took over salt production at the mouth of the River Tiber in 506 BC. Roman soldiers received an allowance to purchase salt, the *salarium,* from where we get the word 'salary'. In the third century BC, a tax on salt was introduced to finance the Second Punic War. Occasional taxes on salt, never high, were exacted at various times throughout the Roman era. It may have been from these beginnings that the idea of raising revenue from salt later took hold in Europe.

Most European countries, at some time, had a Salt Tax of one kind or another. In addition to salt needed purely to survive, vast quantities were used to preserve food. Until modern times, few animals could be fed throughout the winter and were therefore slaughtered in the autumn. To keep them edible, they were salted, or steeped in brine. Fish were similarly preserved, as were some vegetables. Cheap salt, in copious quantities, was essential.

In England, the tax on salt was never really oppressive. Indeed, England was unusual among European countries in

that it had no Salt Tax at all until 1694. However, much of the salt consumed in England before then had been imported, and a small import duty had been introduced in 1303. The importance of this gradually declined as the huge salt deposits in Cheshire and Worcestershire were exploited to make England almost self-sufficient. During the eighteenth century, in general, the tax was kept at a low level. Even so, it was seen as a foreign device and always unpopular. Ironically it was the war against France, at the end of that century, which saw the tax raised to its highest level. William Pitt raised the tax – to thirty times the price of salt – so that a pound of salt was taxed by about one-hundredth of a pound sterling. This was accepted as necessary for the war but, once Napoleon had been defeated, pressure mounted for the tax to be repealed. It was reduced in stages. In 1825 – at a time when the British were imposing the swingeing Salt Tax on more and more people in India – it was finally abolished. It was never reimposed.

Like all taxes on necessities, the Salt Taxes in England bore more heavily on the poor. There were ferocious parliamentary debates over the tax. Its supporters tried to argue that it was a fair tax, since the well off bought more salt for themselves and for their servants. Opponents of the tax spoke of 'the cries of the poor and the wretched', and of legislation 'to grind the face of the poor, in order to relieve a few of the rich'. Parliament was dominated by landowners and, since the alternative to the Salt Tax was a higher tax on property, they voted to tax salt. In peacetime, however, the tax was low. At its highest rate, an English agricultural labourer would have been paying about one per cent of his income to keep his family in necessary salt.

Across the Channel, in France, the history of taxes on salt was very different. It was here that the tax was levied as severely as in India. Wars and revolts mark the history of the French Salt Tax, the notorious *gabelle*. Salt, like other commodities, had previously been taxed as it crossed the domains of individual nobles. Small levies had been made at borders, tollgates, bridges and fords. In the thirteenth century, Charles of Anjou levied a Salt Tax in Provence to finance war. The *gabelle*, however, was levied across France by the central exchequer. It was introduced in 1341, at the beginning of the Hundred Years' War against the English. Like many other taxes, it was supposedly a temporary measure. A few years later it was renewed to raise more money for the army fighting the English, and then again to raise the ransom for the king, Jean II, who had been captured by the Black Prince at Poitier. The *gabelle* soon became a permanent instrument of salt-deprivation and financial oppression.

The *gabelle* was not collected at the same level throughout the domains of the kings of France. In some areas, such as Brittany, the populations were exempt so as to ensure their loyalty. In others, where there were salt pans, the tax was kept moderate to ease its collection. It was in the north, in the provinces of the *grande gabelle,* that the tax revenue was greatest. There, one-third of the country's population paid two-thirds of the total tax burden. The average consumption

of salt in this area dropped to five kilograms a year – half of that in the lesser taxed provinces. Farm animals were denied salt, and this is believed to have permanently depressed agricultural production. Nevertheless, despite all these economies, each peasant's family still lost about six weeks' earnings every year to the *gabelle*. The tax was levied, year in year out, for over four centuries. Moreover, the tax was collected ruthlessly, and with the severest penalties.

An unusual feature of the French tax was that people had to buy a prescribed minimum weekly amount of salt. Failure to do this was an offence. This system of enforcement made collection of the tax considerably easier. The actual collection of the *gabelle* was usually farmed out to the highest bidder. The owners of the rights would then make every effort to maximise their profits. No allowance was made for calamities, such as crop failure. To support the system, the state installed its own inspectors, who were backed up by detachments of the military. Heavy fines were imposed on those who smuggled or otherwise tried to evade the tax. Those who did not, or could not, pay were whipped and imprisoned. In 1680 the penalties were increased. 'Simple contraband' was punished by being sent to the galleys, and 'armed contraband' by death. It is believed that one-third of all French galley slaves had been convicted of salt offences.

The French *gabelle* became notorious across Europe; a byword for oppression. It is not surprising, then, that attempts elsewhere to introduce similar taxes were violently resisted. The seventeenth century brought a revolt in Sicily and, in Piedmont, a four-year 'Salt War'. It was in France itself, however, that the biggest insurrections occurred. In 1548 Henry II tried to impose the *gabelle* in south-west France. These provinces, which produced their own salt, had previously been exempt. Organising through their local communes, the enraged peasants formed their own armies. They laid siege to Angoulême, where the customs men were based. The government was forced to back down, for the time being, and rescind the tax. The peasants became popular heroes across Europe.

There were numerous other rebellions against the tax, particularly in the seventeenth century. Customs men were often driven out of town, had their houses destroyed, or were even killed. For example, as Yves-Marie Berce graphically recounts in *Revolt and Revolution in Early Modern Europe*:

> In July 1658 some salt merchants of Marennes were helping to levy the salt tax at their community's expense. One day they all found notices posted up outside their houses. They assumed that these notices referred to themselves. The notices contained a decree purporting to emanate from the Council, 'to the effect that the Council had sentenced these merchants to be hanged.' The rebels concluded their show of legality by dispatching their victims in certain specially designated execution grounds. They drowned them in a particular well, for example, or hanged them from a gibbet in the public square, or flung them into the river that flowed

past the town. After the execution they disposed of their victims' remains in the prescribed manner. They quartered their bodies and exposed them, and razed their houses to the ground.

Louis XVI, in a last-ditch attempt to avert revolution, abolished the *gabelle* in 1790. Napoleon reintroduced a milder Salt Tax, which was then reduced by Louis XVIII. In 1946 the Salt Tax in France was finally abolished.

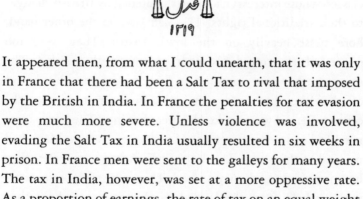

It appeared then, from what I could unearth, that it was only in France that there had been a Salt Tax to rival that imposed by the British in India. In France the penalties for tax evasion were much more severe. Unless violence was involved, evading the Salt Tax in India usually resulted in six weeks in prison. In France men were sent to the galleys for many years. The tax in India, however, was set at a more oppressive rate. As a proportion of earnings, the rate of tax on an equal weight of salt in both the countries was roughly the same. The climate and diseases in India, however, considerably increased the amount of salt necessary to sustain life.

Why was it that the Indian peasants did not rise up in revolt against the Salt Tax like their French counterparts? It has been suggested that 'They accept things that come very much as the will of God', but that seems hardly a sufficient explanation. One reason may be in the peculiar characteristics of salt deprivation. As we have seen, whereas a shortage of water will produce increased thirst, and a shortage of food a sensation of hunger, there is no increased desire for salt when it is withheld, and the physical effects of salt deprivation were often ascribed to other causes. In particular, hunger would mask the effect of salt depletion. Victims would often fail to realise why they felt listless, or worse.

The populace rose up against the British in the 1857 'Indian Mutiny'. That revolt, however, was largely led by the landed classes, whose interests had been threatened by British changes to their traditional rights. The Salt Tax, on the other hand, bore most heavily on the lower castes. They were too oppressed, too cowed, too poor and too weak to rebel. The seventeenth-century peasants in France were poor, but better off than they had been previously. In contrast, nineteenth-century Bengal was wracked by great famines. The lower-caste rural Indians were often on the brink of starvation. Many had no land of their own. Unlike their French counterparts, they had no reserves of money or food. They were too poor to rebel without help from the landed employers upon whom they relied for work. Oppressed by the caste system, they lacked the independence of the French peasant.

For the more wealthy Indian, the high tax on salt would have been an irritation, but things could have been worse – instead of a tax on a minor essential, the British might have levied a tax on their land or their luxuries. It was often suggested that, instead of on salt, a tax should have been placed on sugar. Total consumption of sugar was roughly the same as that of salt. The pattern of consumption, however, was different. Salt was an absolute necessity, so that all required a minimum intake, but it was unpleasant in excess. That resulted in the poor paying almost the same tax as the rich. Sugar, in contrast, was bought with disposable income. The rich consumed much more sugar than the poor. A sugar tax would have borne more heavily on the rich, and lightly on the poor. The destitute would have been exempt.

Collection of a sugar tax would not have been easy, but probably no more difficult than collecting the Salt Tax. The sugar mills would have had to be controlled, similarly to the salt pans and boiling houses. Moreover, there would have been little problem with smuggling from the western borders of the Bengal Presidency, since those territories lacked sugar and imported it from Bengal. A tax on sugar, instead of on salt, could have saved many lives. It would have improved, instead of damaged, the general health. The poor would have been able to purchase the salt needed to protect them from the effects of fever and diarrhoea. It was strongly advocated at parliamentary enquiries into the Salt Tax. As Dr Moore of the Bengal Medical Service put it in his evidence: 'The poorer people cannot get salt.' A duty on sugar 'would come upon a class better able to bear it than those who now pay the duty upon salt'.

That class were unwilling to encourage, or even permit, a revolt against the Salt Tax. For them the Salt Tax was the best alternative. It taxed the poor and left their own wealth intact.

Indeed, some of the larger landowners wanted the land tax reduced and the Salt Tax further increased. That was too much, even for the Viceroy:

> As the representative of the sovereign of India, I regret that such language should have been held to me by the representatives of some of Her Majesty's most favoured Indian subjects, and as the responsible guardian of the general interests of the people of India, I notice with disappointment and surprise, that you, who represent to some extent the wealthiest class in India, whilst deprecating forms of taxation, such as the Bengal Land cesses, which fall mainly on your own class, have not shrunk from advocating and urging on my adoption, other forms of taxation, which fall almost exclusively on the great body of the poor.

The salt monopoly was enforced with the greatest rigour after the Mutiny of 1857. It was only then that the Customs Line became really effective. That, however, was a time when the slightest show of rebellion against British rule would have been instantly repressed, and with maximum force. It was not a good time to consider any protest, let alone one against such an important source of revenue. There had been occasional outbreaks of violence against the Salt Tax earlier in the century, in Orissa and at Surat, but they had been quickly suppressed and had never spread. After the Mutiny, and the establishment of direct British control over India, there

would be no significant rebellion against the Salt Tax until that of Mahatma Gandhi.

Nowadays, when people think of the Indian Salt Tax, they focus on Gandhi's salt march. Vividly depicted in Richard Attenborough's film *Gandhi*, it has etched itself not only on the Indian consciousness, but also that of the world. It was a surprise to me to find that in 1930, at the time of the march, the Salt Tax was relatively low. It stood at $1\frac{1}{4}$ rupees on a *maund* (82 pounds) of salt. The rate inside the Customs Line had been 3 rupees, or more. Moreover, inflation had increased the basic agricultural wage from about 3 rupees a month to nearer 12. The tax burden, therefore, was only about a tenth of what it had been.

When Gandhi selected the Salt Tax as an issue with which to confront the British government it was not an obvious choice. Others in the Indian National Congress were pressing for more popular causes, such as withholding the land tax, marching on Delhi, or setting up a parallel government. They viewed the Salt Tax as a minor issue. Gandhi, however, saw the Salt Tax as manifestly unjust, and difficult for the government to defend:

Next to air and water, salt is perhaps the greatest necessity of life. It is the only condiment of the poor. Cattle cannot live without salt . . . There is no article like salt outside water by taxing which the State can reach even the starving millions, the sick, the maimed and the utterly helpless. The tax constitutes therefore the most inhuman poll tax that ingenuity of man can devise.

But it was part of a larger plan: 'I want to deprive the Government of its illegitimate monopoly of salt. My aim is to get the Salt Tax abolished. That is for me one step, the first step, towards full freedom.' He also saw it as an ideal way to propagate his central philosophy of *satyagraha* – non-violent resistance – as a tool to overcome injustice.

On 12 March 1930, Gandhi and seventy-eight followers set out to break the salt laws. They had been chosen to represent the different castes, religions and regions of India. They would march from their *ashram*, at Sabarmati near Ahmedabad in Gujarat, to the sea at Dandi. There, 241 miles south, they would illegally make salt from the sea. It would be a non-violent protest. They would not seek to defend themselves from attack or arrest.

The journey took twenty-five days. First the volunteers marched through Ahmedabad. At least 100,000 people flocked to see them. Then they marched along a route chosen to pass through villages where there was strong Congress Party support. The villages were close together, and the marchers would often pass through several each day, before stopping in one for the night. At each stop there would be a ceremonial welcome. Gandhi would speak – commonly to a crowd of several thousand. Congress volunteers enrolled; donations to the cause were made. Often the British-appointed headman, the *patel,* who was responsible for tax collection and the local police, resigned his post in sympathy.

The British authorities were caught in a quandary. They wanted to uphold the law – which provided for a fine of 500 rupees or, in default, six months in prison – but did not want to make Gandhi a martyr. Gandhi, of course, was intent on achieving maximum publicity. He had even written to the Viceroy to warn him that the law would be broken. When Gandhi and the marchers set off from their *ashram* they had expected to be arrested almost immediately. The British decided to wait. They hoped the march would fizzle out.

The march towards Dandi, however, was a big success, not only attracting large crowds, but also much publicity from across India and abroad. Nevertheless, the government hesitated. Early on 5 April the salt marchers arrived at the small village of Dandi. On the beach the tide had left pools of water behind, which had evaporated to deposit salt crystals. Gandhi spent the day giving press interviews and speaking to the crowd: 'You can today take the pledge not to eat salt supplied by the government. You have a mine of salt right at your doorsteps.' At six o'clock next morning, Gandhi bathed in the sea. Half an hour later, he walked out of the water to one of the pits where salt had crystallised. He picked some up to symbolically break the law.

The thousands of people gathered with Gandhi then filled

pans with seawater, which they boiled off to make salt. This was sold in little packets to visitors. In the afternoon the police at a nearby village confiscated some manufactured salt, but no arrests were made. Meanwhile the salt laws were being broken under Congress supervision across Gujarat, and at Bombay and Delhi. In the evening, far from Dandi, the police made their first arrests. Over sixty Congress workers were seized, including one of Gandhi's sons.

Over the next weeks agitation increased. There were many arrests, but the illegal manufacture of salt continued all along the Gujarat coast. In addition people refused to pay other taxes. They burnt bonfires of British cloth. However, although Gandhi had been touring to foment resistance, he was still not arrested. At the end of March Gandhi announced a major escalation of the campaign. He urged his followers to support a plan to raid government salt depots, to 'loot the salt-beds of Dharasana, or Bhayander, or Kharaghoda', and to seize the salt of India that he considered the British had unjustly appropriated. On 4 May Gandhi drafted a letter to the Viceroy, to inform him of the intention to raid Dharasana. The decision to detain Gandhi without trial had, however, already been taken. During the night he was arrested and imprisoned.

Gandhi's arrest did not stop the salt raids. On 12 May some of the original Dandi marchers attempted to reach the salt works at Dharasana, and were arrested. A further raid three days later led to severe beatings. On 21 May about 2,500 volunteers gathered at Dharasana. In complete silence they

marched towards the salt heaps. These were surrounded by water-filled ditches, and a barbed wire stockade. Four hundred police, under British officers, and twenty-five riflemen, confronted them. A column of volunteers walked forward. They ignored police orders to disperse. The police rushed on them with steel-tipped *lathis.* The marchers made no effort to ward off the blows. When they had all been beaten to the ground, stretcher-bearers carried them off. Then, column by column, the other volunteers moved forward to receive the same treatment. As the day wore on, the police became more enraged, and often kicked the injured in the stomach or testicles. It was an extremely hot day, and eventually the action was called off. An American journalist there, Webb Miller, counted 320 injured, many with cracked skulls. Two died.

Throughout May there were many other raids on salt depots throughout India. At Wadala, near Bombay, hundreds were arrested and many injured. However, the monsoon was shortly due, when salt production would become impossible. In June the Congress, well satisfied with the publicity achieved, suspended further raids.

Similar tactics were used to enforce the boycott of imported cloth, and encourage non-payment of taxes. Non-violent civil disobedience finally forced the British to release Gandhi and to negotiate with him. A pact between Gandhi and the Viceroy was concluded in March 1931. In return for certain concessions, the Congress agreed to call off its programme of civil disobedience. That included the salt campaign. Gandhi had hoped for abolition of the Salt Tax, but had to settle for only a minor concession – people in the salt-producing areas would be allowed to manufacture salt for their own use. Nevertheless, the confidence and publicity for non-violent action generated by the salt campaign had transformed Indian politics. The Salt Tax, however, would be collected for fifteen more years.

On 2 September 1946 the interim government, which bridged the transition from British rule to independent India, was sworn in. Gandhi was unwilling to speak as it was his weekly day of silence. He handed the new ministers a note to urge the immediate abolition of the Salt Tax. This was finally done, six months before the British left, on 28 February 1947.

TEN

Tamarind Trees

He invented a patent drop for their benefit; so that men
prayed – first that they might be tried by Hume, and
next, if found guilty, they might be hanged by him.

G. O. Trevelyan, *The Competition Wallah*

Private buses were on strike the day we left Jhansi for
Erich. Normally, I was only too happy to travel on the
state buses. Although they were liable to be old and battered,
and the seats none too comfortable, you could be confident
that you would see India out of clear, if not clean, glass.
Private buses tended to have heavily tinted glass. That was
annoying enough but, worst of all, it was often a portent of
finding yourself on a video-bus, damned to non-stop Hindi
films, flickering on a blurred screen, and with the sound
played at horrendous volume.

Nevertheless, it was unfortunate that the private buses were
on strike, as all their passengers were battling for seats, or
even for standing room, on the already over-full state transport and it was several hours before we could push our way on

187

to the Orai bus. Two hours later, halfway to Orai, bruised and aching from the crush, we fought our way off at the village of Punchh. We were five miles from Erich, which lay south-east on the other side of the Betwa River.

The bus strike was also in force at Punchh, and no state buses went on to Erich. Moreover, the private bus crews had persuaded the auto-rickshaw drivers to come out in sympathy. I had just resigned myself to a long walk, when I saw a *tonga*. For a relatively outrageous price, we hired it to go to Erich. Trotting out of town, we gave a lift to a heavily loaded older woman in a gorgeous scarlet sari.

Shortly before Erich, we crossed the Betwa. A massive bridge had been completed only three years before. The river was 200 yards wide, but there were broad sand flats where, during the monsoons, it would have widened to half a mile. Temporary housing had been erected on the flats, which could only have been uncovered a month before, and crops were already sprouting. I was pleased to see that on the far bank there was very little cultivation. The land looked arid. It was covered in thorny acacia trees. With any luck, the Customs Hedge would have been left to grow rampant. Just beyond the bridge, at the outskirts of Erich, we let the woman off, then trotted into the town centre. Erich was small and quite attractive. There were several heavily decorated old mansions, ruined mosques, tombs and a fort. Here and there the old fortified walls still stood, built of huge stones, cleverly cut to interlock without mortar. A great stone gate straddled the main street. We enquired about accommodation, and were told that a *dharamsala* – a hostel for pilgrims – lay next to the post office. We were warned that it might be closed for renovation. And so it was.

The post office was wonderfully old-fashioned. A small lobby contained the counter, but most people went into the office behind, presided over by the amiable Laxman Singh Jehlot. Worn and dusty files bulged out of dark wooden cupboards; an assistant dripped molten wax on to mailbag ties and impressed an official seal.

Laxman Singh sent for glasses of tea. I explained about our quest for the Customs Hedge. Neither he, nor any of the customers or onlookers, knew anything helpful.

'Where can we stay?' I enquired.

'There's nowhere, nowhere at all.'

'Come now,' I protested, 'there must be somewhere we can get a room. I have stayed in villages all over India.' I took out some money. 'There must be somewhere.'

'It's not a question of money,' he chided me softly, 'there is just no space in this town. I was transferred here recently, and had to spend the first four months sleeping on the post office floor.'

'So, what can we do?'

'I don't know. What can you do?'

'What do you think we should do?' I countered, determined to stay in Erich.

'Well,' he looked over the top of his cracked spectacles, 'we could phone the Chairman of the Council, and ask him what to do. Shall I do that?'

'Yes, why not?'

Relieved to be shifting the responsibility for the well-being of this persistent foreigner, he sprang into action, and was soon conducting a telephone conversation in animated and rapid Hindi. Several minutes later he replaced the phone.

'Well?' I asked eagerly.

'He was out.'

'Where? When will he be back?'

'No one knows. I left a message for him to telephone me.'

'Do you think that will be soon?'

'Probably not.'

We sat in silence. Occasionally one of us looked at the phone. Half an hour passed, and the crowd of onlookers thinned out.

'You could go and see the ex-Chairman of the Council,' the postmaster suggested.

'Will he be able to find us accommodation?'

'No, but he is very interested in history. He might know about the Customs Line.'

I left Santosh to look after our bags and await any telephone call. Two schoolboys were instructed to guide me. It was further than I had supposed. We climbed up steep streets, out through another of the ancient stone gateways, then along a track into the dense acacia trees above the town. We passed a huge well, topped with four massive pillars. We climbed again, and there, amid the green bushes, was the house. It was large and bright blue.

We walked up to the great portico, resplendent with

190

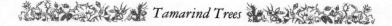

fretted stonework, niches, pillars, and arches. Orange Hindi script on either side of the doorway read *shubh* and *laabh*, the words for 'luck' and 'well-being'. Invocations to Laxshmi and Ganesh were punctuated with lucky swastikas. As we approached the great brass-studded door, a lady in a scarlet sari emerged. It was the same woman we had given a lift to. She put her palms together in greeting, and called to her husband.

Hardas Verma was an imposing man. Physically not particularly large, he had an air of quiet authority. On the brink of old age, he held himself well. His thick smoothed-back hair was a perfect white. I explained why I was in Erich. He appeared to know nothing about the Customs Line.

'And,' I continued, 'we are waiting to hear from the Chairman of the Council, as to whether he can find us anywhere to stay.'

'Don't worry about him. You come and stay here, with me.'

I discovered later that the two men were arch-rivals. Hardas Verma had been Chairman of the Council for many years, until he had been supplanted by the candidate of the relatively new Bharatiya Janata Party, the BJP, which had swept to power across the state of Uttar Pradesh. The strange thing was that the BJP, the Hindu nationalist party, normally attracted the support of the traditional land-owning class, but Hardas Verma had represented the Samajwadi Party, the socialists.

I collected Santosh from the post office. Everyone there was delighted, and relieved, that we had found accommodation. The Chairman had not phoned back, and he never did. Santosh got on very well with the Vermas. Hardas Verma's wife, Surya Mukhi, came from near Santosh's village, and she soon established that they knew people in common. The Vermas had been *zamindars* of Erich. Rather like English eighteenth-century squires, they had owned the village and the surrounding agricultural land. Indeed, the British had deliberately copied the English system, installing the Mughal tax collectors as owners of the land, so as to facilitate the collection of the land taxes. The concept of ownership allowed the administration to confiscate the estates of those who failed to collect the taxes, take what was owed, and then sell the land to those more efficient or more ruthless. As a young man, Hardas Verma had inherited the family property. In the land reforms that followed independence, 'they stole my land,' he told me. However, he and his family were left with forty acres to farm, a couple of labourers' cottages, and the vast house. This left them still relatively wealthy.

The house was not so spacious as it seemed. Despite covering much land, and rising to three storeys of galleried outer walls, the open centre resulted in there being very little in the way of rooms. Santosh and I were offered a disused room in a corner tower, but it looked very bleak. We ended up sleeping in the large reception room, just inside the great door, together with Hardas Verma and his son. The women and grandchildren were in rooms next to the kitchen, on the far side of the massive internal courtyard.

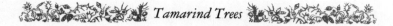

Before we went to bed, I talked again of the Customs Line, and of my search for its remains. Vermaji had absolutely no knowledge of where it might be, or even that it had existed. As his family had been in Erich for 300 years and had been the landowners, this was discouraging. What was more, he was completely baffled as to why the Customs Line should be of any interest to me or to anyone else. He, himself, was interested in the remains of ancient civilisations – millennia-old terracotta figures, and inscriptions in forgotten scripts – that had been discovered locally. My researches into the remains of the Raj, he thought, were hardly 'history'.

'Even if you find your hedge,' he said mournfully, 'what will be the point?' After the oil-lamps were extinguished, I lay awake for a long time on the too short *charpoy*. I felt rather dispirited. Perhaps it was all a waste of time.

We were up at dawn. I climbed the three tiers of stone steps from the courtyard to the walkway on top of the three-foot-thick walls. I watched the sun rise and hit Erich. The sky was crystal clear. I felt refreshed, and optimistic. A pair of pink hoopoes wheeled over the acacia bushes. Workers came to get their instructions for the day, while we breakfasted on *chapatis* and buffalo yoghurt.

A monk from the nearby Hanuman Temple arrived. He had a bushy white beard and wore a long red gown. He was old, but still powerfully built. He chatted to Hardas Verma for a while, then he turned to me.

'I hear you are searching for the Old Line,' he said.

'That's right, do you know anything about if?'

'Yes.' He sipped at a cup of tea, then casually added, 'Finish your breakfast, and I'll take you there.'

It was difficult to take in. After years of searching, I had finally met someone who had not only heard of the Customs Line, but also claimed to know where it was. I steeled myself for another disappointment. Maybe he was talking of an old boundary.

'Which way does the line go?' I asked.

'From Erich north, towards the River Betwa.'

'Right,' I said, for it sounded good, 'let's go.'

I took out my old maps, and worked out the longitude and latitude of where the Customs Line was shown as crossing the Betwa River. I set my satellite navigator. I wanted to be able to see how closely the monk's 'Old Line' was to the 'Customs Line' depicted on the map of 1874. The three of us – Santosh, myself, and the monk, Radesham Pujari – set off, skirting the east of Erich until we hit the main road back to Punchh. We walked down to a junction, where another tarred road went south.

'That,' Radesham Pujari said, 'is the road that goes to Chirgaon, where it meets the main road from Punchh to Jhansi. It was built on top of the Old Line.' He turned around to face north. 'On the other side you can see the Old Line going off to Konch. That *imli* tree marks the beginning. There used to be a row of them all along the line.'

A magnificent old tamarind tree stood on the other side of the main road. Underneath I could see a narrow sandy track, which went off north across the fields. We climbed down from the road to follow it.

In some ways I was disappointed that so little was left of the Customs Line. Nevertheless, it was exciting to at last be walking alongside what did remain; to be following the steps of the old customs officers. People had widened their fields to encroach on the line and occasionally we lost the track completely or came to a divided path. The monk would call out to people tending their crops to enquire as to the where-abouts of the 'Old Line', and we would be put straight. They all seemed to be familiar with it. On every side the land was cultivated. I cursed my luck that where the Customs Line ran through the uncultivated country, south of Erich, it had been buried beneath a road; that here, where there was no road, it had been largely destroyed by farming.

I saw an old building, all covered in creepers. 'Could that be an old customs house?' I asked eagerly.

'No,' the monk replied, giving me a strange look, 'it's the old Raja's elephant stables.'

We walked for about two hours. It became very hot. Some bushes with red berries lined the track. The monk and Santosh picked some and gave me a handful. They tasted sharp but fruity.

'What are they called?' I asked.

'*Ber*.'

I looked down and saw that the bushes were covered in vicious spikes. I suddenly realised that this was the Indian plum, the principal thorn-bush of the Customs Hedge.

Possibly it was a re-seeding from one of the original bushes. We passed another tamarind tree. I was assured that the tamarinds were probably well over a hundred years old. If so, then they were perhaps the only original trees left, for I remembered Dr Dutt of the National Remote Sensing Agency telling me that none of those trees listed in the Annual Reports has a life span of more than sixty years. Tamarind trees have no thorns, so why had they been planted? Perhaps it had been to provide an anchor for the original cut-thorn barrier; perhaps it had been for the dense evergreen foliage to give shade to the patrolling officers.

We reached the bank of the River Betwa. In the rains it must have been very impressive, for the other bank was hundreds of yards away. As it was, shallow streams ran across sandy flats. Unfortunately, the water was still too deep to make a crossing. Radesham Pujari told me that the track of the Old Line continued on the other side for a while, before a road to Konch buried it. I took a reading on my GPS navigator. We were at 25°49.2'N, 79°07.0'E. From the 1874 map I had calculated the Customs Line as meeting the Betwa River at 25°49.5'N, 79°06.5'E. That was only half a mile to the west. Considering the 1874 map was only on a scale of one inch to every eight miles, it was amazingly close.

We retraced our way back to Erich. I plucked samples from the trees on the Customs Line, which later I would press and frame to adorn the walls of my London flat. I took photographs of the Customs Line, and of Radesham Pujari pointing to the tamarind trees, Indian plum bushes, and other features. I gave him some money for all his help.

'You're a monk at a temple in Erich, aren't you?'

'Yes, at Lord Hanuman's shrine.'

'So, how do you know all this terrain so well?'

'Well, I wasn't always a monk.'

'What did you used to do?'

'I was a *dacoit*.'

'A *dacoit*! A bandit?' I wondered whether I had correctly understood the monk's Hindi.

'Yes, I was a *dacoit* for many years. Look!' He rolled up his red gown, and exposed his thighs and back. He was covered in scars. 'Bullet holes.'

'What happened?'

'The police ambushed us. I was in jail from 1968 to 1979, so I had plenty of time to think about the future. When I was released, I changed professions. I became a monk.'

'You were a bandit around here?'

'Yes, that's why I know the area so well. However,' his eyes twinkled, 'it looked a bit different on horseback at night.'

We collected our belongings from Vermaji's house. He was very pleased that I was so happy, although still at a loss as to why I was so delighted to have found the Customs Line.

'What is the point?' he lamented. 'What is the use?'

We had lunch and packed. I did not want to impose further on the Vermas, and we needed to leave quickly to reach Jhansi by nightfall. I took photographs of all the family. I also hurried to the post office, and took some photographs of the helpful postmaster. I promised to write from London, and send all of them prints. The bus and auto-rickshaw strike was still in progress, but the Vermas were confident we could find a *tonga*. Their tractor was going to a field on the other side of town, so we clambered on top of the seed drill to get a lift to the crossroads.

As our *tonga* clattered towards Punchh, I considered what we had seen. I was, of course, delighted to have at last found something. I was totally confident that I had seen the remnants of the Customs Hedge. Nevertheless, I would have liked to have found more than a narrow track and a few old trees. It was true that people still referred to the path as the 'Old Line', however no one had seemed to know of its origin, of its association with the Salt Tax. I wondered why this was so. Maybe it was because Erich lay on the wrong side of the Customs Line, or rather on the right side – for the line had been taken around Erich. Its residents had been exempt from the draconian tax. The Customs Line would only have been an inconvenience for them. Perhaps in Etawah, where people had lived inside the line of the hedge, there might be stronger memories.

'Do you think we should go on to Etawah?' I asked Santosh.

'Yes, yes,' he said eagerly, 'let's go.'

'You don't think you ought to return to your family in Gwalior?'

'No. Let's go to Etawah.'

'But you said you thought Etawah might be dangerous, didn't you?'

'Maybe, but I'm in no hurry to get back to Gwalior.'

'What do you mean?'

Then it came out. I found out why Santosh had not been his usual cheerful self. He told me that his family had found a bride for him. They had even given her some jewellery to further matters. He, however, had refused to have anything to do with it; had declined even to meet her. His family was really angry with him.

'But why didn't you want to meet her?' I asked. 'Did you hear she wasn't pretty? Are you interested in someone else?'

'No. Not at all. Apparently she's beautiful, and her family are wealthy.'

'So?'

'I'm too young,' he said, looking miserable. 'I'm too young to get married.'

'Right.' I gave him a big smile. 'Perhaps you are. Let's go to Etawah.'

I was happy to make one final effort. We would explore the land between the Rivers Yamuna and Chambal. Perhaps there, in Etawah District, we would find more than we had at Erich.

It seemed fitting that my final effort to find the Customs Hedge would be in the district once ruled by the man who had made it so formidable. Allan Octavian Hume was an extraordinary man. He had followed his father into the East India Company's service, and joined the Bengal Civil Service in 1849. After a few minor jobs, he was placed in charge of Etawah District as Magistrate and Collector. Not unusually for the time, he was only twenty-six. He was still there two years later when the Mutiny broke out, and rebels took Etawah town. He led sorties against them, raised local levies, and fought with the artillery at Agra. Hume then led 300 riflemen to recapture Etawah. Afterwards, he appears to have behaved relatively well, if a little eccentrically. In *The Competition Wallah,* published just after the Mutiny, G. O. Trevelyan wrote:

> Mr Hume of Etawah who was blamed by many for excess of leniency, but who so bore himself that no one could blame him for want of courage, distinguished himself by keeping down the number of executions in his district to seven, and by granting the culprits a fair trial. These he treated with fatherly tenderness, for he invented a patent drop for their benefit; so that men prayed – first, that they might be tried by Hume, and next, if found guilty, they might be hanged by him.

Hume was passionately interested in birds. He must have been delighted to have been appointed Commissioner of

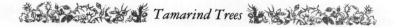

Inland Customs, for the great Customs Hedge offered unrivalled opportunities to enlarge his collection of specimens. The men he appointed – 'young men fond of sport . . . who can do their work as well, if not better, gun in hand' – were eager to help. He left his collection of 63,000 birds and 15,500 eggs to the Natural History Museum in London. It was there that I saw his diaries. Only one of them, that for 1867, covered Hume's time as Commissioner. It was a catalogue of slaughter. Some days dozens of birds were shot, often for just a single specimen. Only one diary entry mentioned the barrier he was supervising:

> 27 Nov. To Replee 11 miles. This was formerly an Ass Patrol's Post. It is now broken up and the nearest post is Odha 7 miles further – in this neighbourhood Mr Conway kills immense numbers of deer in pitfalls behind the line hedge – sometimes 19 or 20 are taken in one night in a single pitfall both Antelope and Ravine Deer – the place at which they usually jump the hedge is soon seen & a pitfall is dug just where they alight.

Hume received official praise for his work in making the Customs Line so effective. He was promoted to be Secretary to the Government of India, and afterwards headed a new Department of Revenue, Agriculture and Commerce. However, when he began to urge some liberal reforms he was transferred to finish his years in a backwater at the Board of Revenue.

Hume's later life was amazingly different – so much so that the latest biography of him is in a series on Indian freedom fighters. He became interested in theosophy, a religion influenced by Hinduism and Buddhism, and developed sympathies towards Indian culture and aspirations. When he retired from the Civil Service in 1882 he decided to stay in India. He became friendly with Indians who wanted more say in how their country was governed. In 1883 he wrote an open letter to the 'Graduates of Calcutta University', urging the establishment of an association to further the political advancement of educated Indians. He was anxious for Indians to take the initiative, and for European sympathisers to have a subordinate role. However, it was Hume himself who organised the first national meeting in 1885, at which the Indian National Congress was formed, and it was Hume who became the first General Secretary of the Congress. He dominated the Congress for the next twenty-five years. It would become the party that Mahatma Gandhi would lead to take India to freedom, and the party that would rule independent India for many years.

On my last night in the Jhansi Hotel I lay awake thinking about the trip to Etawah. I was on the edge of sleep. I began to wonder what Hume would have made of my quest. Given his sympathies, would he have wanted the oppressive Customs Hedge he built to have disappeared without trace, or would he have wanted a fragment to be left as a reminder of those times, would he . . . No, it was nonsense. I emptied my mind, and slept.

The Chambal

*The physical features of Etawah, which rendered it
practically inaccessible in earlier times, marked it out for
many ages as a secure retreat for the lawless and
turbulent.*

The Imperial Gazetteer of India, 1881

The confluence of the Yamuna and Chambal Rivers is in
Etawah District. It took us only four hours by bus to
reach Etawah town. We travelled via Gwalior, but did not
leave the bus station. I did not want to waste time, and
Santosh was in no hurry to meet his family. The road crossed
the Chambal first, then ran through five miles of rugged
terrain to the Yamuna River, where it bordered the town of
Etawah. The 1876 map of 'Etawa' showed the Customs Line
running south-east from Agra District down between the two
rivers. Although I had earmarked a portion of the line further
south-east as being more hopeful, I nevertheless scrutinised
the landscape carefully once we had crossed the Chambal.

In India, the word 'Chambal' is immediately associated

with bandits, the notorious Chambal *dacoits*. For centuries these *dacoits* have operated from the valley of the river and the surrounding ravines. It was also the home of the infamous *thuggies*, the hereditary murderers, who befriended travellers, then strangled them in their sleep. It was Colonel Sleeman, who had written the book in which I had first read of the Customs Hedge, who had suppressed their activities. Every year, all over northern India, they had killed hundreds of men, women and children. An old gazetteer records that in Etawah 'in one year [1808] sixty-seven dead bodies were taken out of wells in this district.' In recent years the ravines have been home to the legendary *dacoit* Dau Mansingh, and to the 'Bandit Queen', Phoolan Devi. At the time of my visit I read in the newspapers that the police were hunting 'Haribaba, who is carrying a reward of Rs 50,000 on his head, and wanted in connection with two dozen cases'.

I had imagined a landscape of vast plateaux and canyons, like those in Arizona. The Chambal ravines were actually much more modest. The sandy terrain was washed away into a series of gorges, at most a hundred feet deep. Much of the land was covered in thorny acacias. At first I was disappointed, and slightly incredulous that the authorities had been so thwarted in their searches for the bandits. Later, after mile upon mile of the narrow ravines, I began to realise how difficult it would be to find anyone hidden there. It was a gigantic random maze.

We passed through the small town of Udi, where we crossed a road running between the two rivers. It struck me that it could possibly be over the old Customs Line. A bus lay on its

side against the road, its roof completely ripped off. Grey-mantled crows were scouring the inside. A few miles later we were in Etawah town. It was a dreary place. Most of the buildings needed repair. Despite it being a Sunday, an incredible number of lorries jammed the streets, where they belched out black diesel fumes. A. O. Hume, whose administration was commemorated by a bazaar still known as Humeganj, would not have been pleased. However, I thanked my luck that I was there in November, and not a few months later, during the hot winds, when, as one nineteenth-century visitor wrote:

Every article of furniture is burning to the touch; the hardest wood, if not well covered with blankets, will split with a report like that of a pistol; and linen taken from the drawers is as if just removed from a kitchen fire. The nights are terrible, every apartment being heated to excess, each may be compared to a large oven.

As it was, the weather was perfect – with low humidity, moderate temperature and, apart from the pollution, clear blue skies. We checked into a small hotel, had a quick lunch, and took the Kanpur bus to Bakewar. There were no motor vehicles for hire, so we took a *tonga.* The driver, Shabir, was extremely jovial and helpful. He and his horse, Raja, normally plied the road we wanted – first to Lakhna, and then over the Yamuna to Chakanagar. The 1876 map of Etawah District showed the Customs Line as passing right through the middle of Chakanagar.

We trotted off in the two-wheeled buggy at a brisk pace. Shabir was very proud of Raja, and urged him on with a continual Hindi commentary. 'Steady, steady . . . faster here . . . relax, relax . . . slower up the hill . . . watch this bend . . . faster now . . . steady, steady . . . well done Raja . . .' Shabir assured us that his horse – in much better condition than the ones we had hired in Erich – could do sixty miles a day. Every mile or so, at a crossroads or group of houses, Raja would suddenly stop, then have to be coaxed on. Those were the places where he normally dropped off, or took on, passengers, and where he was used to a short rest.

It was seven miles to the bridge over the Yamuna. Before the river, we passed through a landscape of small cultivated fields. Women in bright saris, *ornis* covering their heads, were weeding. Occasionally, one of them would draw her *orni* across her face then turn to look at us. The road was good and, until the river, lined on both sides with fine old trees. Beyond the bridge the country was wild. We had to stop at a tollgate, where Shabir took the bucket that hung below the *tonga* and pumped water into it for the horse. I climbed an embankment to survey the surrounding country. It was covered with crumbling hills and narrow ravines. There was no sign of cultivation or habitation. We cantered on.

Chakanagar was bigger than I had expected. It had a bank, police station, and even an off-licence, a 'Country Wine Bar', where liquor was pushed out through a tiny hole in a formidable mesh front. We stopped at the crossroads in the centre of town for a glass of tea. Soon the little stall,

208

with its two outside benches, was crowded with onlookers. It seemed that foreigners were rare. Everyone was curious to know why we were in Chakanagar, and we were keen to talk. No one, however, seemed to know about the Customs Line.

An older man, Naubal Singh, with shaved head and a conspicuous red *tilak* on his forehead, arrived. He was obviously held in some respect, for the crowd gave way for him. I explained our quest.

'Aree!' he exclaimed. 'You are looking for the *Parmat Lain?*'

I immediately recognised the Hindi words. They were the same ones that had been written, in Devanagari script, against the Customs Line on the 1870 map of Jalaun District that I had seen in the India Office Library two years ago.

'Yes! Yes! We're looking for the *Parmat Lain.*'

'It used to come right through here,' he said.

'Yes, yes, I know. But where is it?'

'Ahh.' He pointed to the crossroads. 'It was over there. In the 1940s they built the road from Udi to Bhareh right over the top of it.'

'But is there nothing left?'

'Nothing. Nothing at all.'

'No trees?'

'Nothing.'

I was glad to have found someone with memories of the Customs Line, but very disappointed to discover that the hedge seemed to have been obliterated. We continued to talk for a while, but the old man was positive that nothing remained. As in so many other places, the old line had been a boon to the planners of roads. It was obvious, I now realised, that the swathe that had been cut across India was ideal for road construction. It usually linked towns and, in addition, the Customs Line was often raised to facilitate observation across country. That would drain water away from a road during the monsoons. Moreover, often being free from cultivation, it would have been cheap to build upon.

'It's getting late,' Naubal Singh warned. 'You should think about going. This area is full of *dacoits*. The roads around here are very dangerous after dark.'

The sky was already coloured with the setting sun. I went to pay my bill at the tea stall, but the owner, perhaps because we had attracted so much business, waved me away. We thanked everyone profusely, climbed into our *tonga*, and sped off. The birds had settled for the night, and the ravines were ominously quiet. The tollgate keeper urged us to hurry. We reached the Yamuna bridge just in time to see the sun dip into the river.

North of the Yamuna, I felt safe again. Workers were leaving their fields to return home. The dust from bullock carts hung in the air. A huge flock of sheep on the road slowed our progress. I told Shabir to stop for a moment beneath a vast banyan tree. The leaves of the banyan are used to make disposable plates – two or more of the dried leaves being pressed into shape and tacked together with thorns. Ecologically minded friends in Spain had asked me to bring them some seeds. In the half-light, Santosh, Shabir and I searched for banyan 'figs'. It was not the season, but we found a couple.

Under the great tree there was a Shiva shrine, with ancient terracotta figures of the god and his consort Durga. Someone had lit an oil-lamp and sprinkled the figures with hibiscus flowers. I offered up a prayer.

The sheep had disappeared down a side road. We clattered on towards Lakhna and Bakewar. Santosh and Shabir chattered away up front, while Raja needed no urging now he was going home. The air was getting cold, and I put a shawl around my shoulders. I thought about what I should do.

I was at the last of the sites I had selected. The Agra section of the Customs Line seemed to have been ploughed up. Nothing appeared to have survived in Jalaun District. Nothing was to be seen near Jhansi town. The Babina section was a military range. It was true I had found some remnants at Erich, but those were less than I had hoped for. It might be that in the future I would find some large-scale map showing every detail of the Customs Line, which would enable me to follow its every twist and turn. That, however, seemed unlikely. Perhaps, also in the future, satellite imaging would enable a minute examination of all the possible terrain. That also seemed wishful thinking and, in any case, too far removed from the present. I had nowhere else to turn. Should I accept what I had been told at Chakanagar – that every vestige of the Customs Hedge there had been destroyed – and call it a day?

'What do you think, Santosh,' I asked. 'Do you want to go home tomorrow, or should we return to Chakanagar?'

'Go home!' The possibility had obviously never occurred to him. He spoke with youthful enthusiasm. 'Of course not! We must carry on looking. Naubal Singh could be mistaken. Remember what happened at Erich – there, at first, everybody told us there was no Customs Line.'

'That's right,' Shabir chipped in. 'And you'll have me as a guide.'

Their zeal was infectious. I put my earlier doubts down to tiredness. By the time we reached Bakewar, we had arranged to meet Shabir there the next day at nine o'clock. From there we would go back to Chakanagar, and travel beyond.

On the Monday, Santosh and I returned to Bakewar. When we got down from the bus, Shabir was waiting for us. We had tea together and agreed terms to hire the *tonga* for the day. I had assumed he owned the *tonga* himself but he told us that, like others in the town, both the carriage and horse were owned by a rich businessman, the *malik*. I was shocked to learn that he only paid Shabir 30 rupees a day. We came to a deal, whereby I would pay the hire charge, but give some extra money to Shabir. I promised that in no circumstances would I tell the *malik*, who otherwise would take it for himself.

The previous evening, I had consulted my maps and worked out a plan of action. I decided to ignore the section of the Customs Line that ran from Chakanagar north-west to Udi. I

had seen the tar road leave Chakanagar and, travelling from Gwalior to Etawah, what looked like the same road arriving at Udi. It seemed likely that its construction would have obliterated any remnants of the Customs Line. I had opted, therefore, to concentrate my efforts on the section running south-east from Chakanagar. The road going in that direction, from the crossroads at Chakanagar, was signposted to Bhareh – a town ten miles away, near to where the Yamuna and the Chambal Rivers met. The Customs Line on the 1876 map, however, was shown as swinging south to cross the Chambal only five miles from Chakanagar. It seemed possible that the new road and the Customs Line diverged a few miles out of Chakanagar, and perhaps from there the Customs Line was intact.

I had in mind what we had done in Erich. I had similarly calculated the longitude and latitude of where the Customs Line crossed the river. The difference would be that we would walk up the river to find the spot. It should, I reasoned, prove easier than traversing the ravines.

'Yes,' Santosh concurred, 'and, with *dacoits* hiding in the jungle, a good deal safer too!'

We made good time to Chakanagar. Raja seemed to be getting used to his new role, and only occasionally halted at his traditional stops. We took tea at the crossroad stall. People there were surprised to see us back, and sceptical of our mission. Naubal Singh came to join us.

'But the *Parmat Lain* was completely buried by the road,' he protested. 'Fifty years ago!'

'Perhaps,' I said.

213

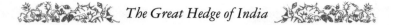

We carried on through the town to the Chambal River. It was only a couple of miles. At first there were fields, but soon these gave way to thorn bushes and ravines. The river was about a third of a mile wide. Piers were being built across from the far bank to take a new bridge, but there was no sign of activity. Wide banks of dried mud showed that the river had been in flood quite recently. Now, however, there was hardly a current. There was no wind. The water lay dark and flat.

I looked downstream but, because of bends, could only see a mile or so. There were occasional patches of cultivated land, but no signs of habitation. We left Shabir behind to wait for us, then, thinking the mud-banks might be soft, we started to walk along the top of the riverbank. The route was so tortuous, however, and so obstructed by thorn trees, that we soon decided to risk descending to the flats. They turned out to be reasonably firm. Later on they became hard and crazed, broken into tiles a foot across, with deep crevices in-between. We had to make frequent detours to circumvent creeks and quagmires. It was clear that we should have to walk a good deal further than the five miles I had calculated. I switched on my satellite navigator. As we walked, I watched the miles to our destination decrease almost imperceptibly. It was hot and I was only carrying a litre of water. I had been stupid not to bring water-purification tablets.

It was eerily quiet. There was not a person to be seen. There were no boats; no fishing nets. Nor was there much bird life – only the occasional cormorant or pied kingfisher. We walked

for two hours without meeting anyone. I was all for making
forays into the interior, to see if we could find somebody to ask
about the Customs Line. Santosh was not so keen since he was
convinced the place was teeming with *dacoits*. We were only a
mile from our destination when we saw an old man tending
his goats on the brow of the embankment. White-mous-
tached, he was dressed all in white too, with a voluminous
dhoti hanging down like plus fours. His bulky turban was tied
so that the tail hung down to cover his neck. He was tall, and
carried a bamboo staff twice his height. We climbed up the
bank to talk with him. After we had exchanged greeting, he
told us his name was Dhaman Singh and that he was eighty.

'Is there a big thorn hedge near here?' I asked him. 'We are
looking for the barrier the British built to collect the Salt
Tax.'

'No,' he replied firmly, 'there's nothing here like that.'

'Are you sure? I have an old map showing the *Parmat Lain*
running very close to here.'

'Ah, the *Parmat Lain*. Why didn't you say so? Yes,' he
gestured further down the river, 'the *Parmat Lain* used to
come from Chakanagar to Pali Ghar.'

'And where's that?'

'About a mile downstream.'

'And what remains of the *Parmat Lain*?'

'Oh, nothing! They covered it with a road in Indira
Gandhi's time.'

'There's nothing left?'

'Nothing at all.'

215

Dispirited, we pressed on. Mrs Gandhi had been assassinated while Prime Minister in 1984, so it seemed unlikely that any vestiges of hedge would have survived. I might have been tempted to return to the *tonga* at this point, had we not come so far. As it was, I thought it would be easier to go on to Pali Ghar, and then walk back to Chakanagar on the very road that covered the Customs Line. It turned out to be much more than a mile. I was terribly thirsty. Eventually, we saw a heavily used track leading down to the river. We climbed up it and saw the village of Pali Ghar before us.

Our arrival caused quite a stir. People looked on amazed as we ascended the track that led past the temple into the centre of the village. A group of old men, sitting in the shade of a veranda, beckoned. I walked over, as casually as I could, and raised my joined palms.

'*Namaskar*,' I greeted them.

'*Namaskar*,' they replied. Then a chorus of voices, 'Where are you from?'

'Why are you here?'

I left it to Santosh to explain about our search, in his proper Hindi. We were invited to sit with the men, and tea was sent for. Meanwhile, I drank beaker upon beaker of water. Beyond the veranda, women looked at us surreptitiously, their faces covered. Children pressed close. One old man turned out to speak fair English, so we started a parallel conversation.

'You walked here along the bank of the Chambal?' he asked incredulously.

'Yes, there seemed to be no other way. I had thought we

might get a lift on a boat, but there were none on the river. Why was that?'

'Why?' He looked at me pityingly. 'Why? Because it's dangerous, that's why. Boats get shot up by the *dacoits*. It's very risky to go about on your own anywhere near here.'

'But you live safely out here in the village.'

'Yes, but we know what's going on, and,' he added forcefully, 'we've got guns!'

'Ah.'

Tea arrived – special tea for guests, with double the normal, already generous, quantity of sugar. I carried on talking to the English speaker, P. S. Chauvan, who turned out to be a retired college principal with an MA in geography.

'So, I understand you're looking for the *Parmat Lain?*' he said.

'You know it?'

'Oh, yes. It ran from here to Chakanagar. But they built the road on top of it years ago.'

'Is nothing left?'

'Oh, yes. You can still see some of it. Before the road starts, on the edge of the village.'

'Can you take us there?' I asked, already rising to my feet.

'Yes, yes.' He gestured for me to sit down. 'We'll take you there. But, have a biscuit first.'

A tray of biscuits was handed around. I took one. It had the word 'Britannia' stamped on the face.

'Let's go,' said Chauvanji.

Accompanied by some of the old men, we walked away

from the river to the edge of the village. There, between the fields, ran a narrow strip of grassy land. It was slightly raised, and about twenty feet wide.

'The *Parmat Lain*!' Chauvanji announced proudly.

'People have been nibbling away at it,' someone said with a chuckle, 'it used to be at least twice the width.'

To others it might not have been impressive, but for me it was the end of a long and arduous search. I was filled with joy, and relief. Here it was, at last – the Customs Line. I walked up and stood on top, as though I were king of the castle. The villagers looked bemused. Santosh took my photo. Then I took photographs of Santosh, of Chauvanji, and of all the other villagers with us. I took out my satellite navigator and made a reading. We were at 26°32.2'N, 79°09.2'E. Compared with what I had calculated from the map of 1876, we were on exactly the same latitude, and only one minute of longitude, about one mile, further east. It was a triumph, both for me, and for the Victorian cartographers. Nevertheless, accurate as my predictions were, I should never have found the eroded Customs Line without the help of the villagers.

'Further on,' Mr Chauvan pointed across the fields, 'it's more impressive.' We followed the Customs Line north. Sometimes we had to walk around stacked sheaves of grain. Sometimes the encroachments almost met, leaving the narrowest of footpaths. However, the raised camber of the line, even when cultivated, was always visible. Soon we were into uncultivated country. The other men drifted back to the village, and left Chauvanji to guide us. In immaculately ironed white shirt, and long checked *dhoti*, he strode confidently along the raised footpath. Although bald and ageing, he was remarkably fit.

Suddenly, to my surprise and delight, the Customs Line became a Customs Hedge. Clusters of thorny acacias topped the embankment. Some were twenty feet high. Thorn-covered Indian plum trees barred the way. It was impossible to tell whether the trees were original or re-seedings. Whichever they were, it was the Customs Hedge. We had found it at last. Laughing, Santosh and I posed for more photographs.

The embankment was fully forty feet wide, and well raised. A lot of earth must have been moved to create it. After a few hundred yards, the hedge petered out as it ran into a low hill of crumbling sand dunes. Rather than cross them, the Customs Line, instead of being raised above the country, became a deep cutting. With steep walls, twenty feet high, and men patrolling below, it would have been a formidable barrier. On the other side of the hill, it reverted to being a raised bank for a few hundred yards, before joining the tarred road from Bhareh to Chakanagar. There, all signs of its passage had been obliterated.

'Were there no customs buildings?' I asked Chauvanji.

'Nothing solid – or so the old men told me when I was young. Just flimsy *chowkies*.'

'Did they tell you anything else?'

'Probably. They used to carry on about the high price of salt. But, of course, being young, we didn't take much notice of their moans.' He laughed. 'Just like now, when the young don't want to hear me talk of the old days. One thing I do remember, though – they used to talk about how the customs men were so close together along the *Parmat Lain*, that they could shout to each other. They used to be able to relay a message from here to Jhansi, and even to Agra, and some said even to Delhi.'

'With the price of salt so high, didn't people smuggle it across the Customs Line?'

'It was too well guarded, and there were fines and imprisonment if you were caught. They just had to suffer. But, occasionally, a large band of Maratha smugglers would break through the *Parmat Lain* on camels. Later, on their return, they would breach it again, smuggling sugar and tobacco the other way. But that didn't help the people in Pali Ghar. Look!'

Until then, I had seen no camels in the area but, as if on cue, a huge male camel came lumbering down the road with a heavy load on its back. We laughed, and gave greetings to the driver who led it – a thuggish-looking young man, wearing jeans, a white bandanna around his forehead, and a tee-shirt emblazoned 'Polo'.

It was time to go. We waited at the side of the road, from where there was regular transport to Chakanagar. I thanked Chauvanji for all his help, and promised to write.

'You go home,' I urged him, for he was on his own now. 'We'll be fine.'

'Not at all. You've been very lucky so far. It's my duty to wait with you, and see you off safely.'

'We'll be all right. Really.'

'No. And remember,' he pointed towards Bhareh, 'don't think of looking for the *Parmat Lain* east of here. There, it is even more dangerous. You will definitely be killed!'

A three-wheeled *tempo*, chugging black smoke, came into view. Chauvanji waved it down, and Santosh and I climbed in. We pulled away.

'Thanks,' I shouted, 'thanks a lot.'

'Have a good journey,' he shouted back. 'You came just in time. The Public Works Department men were in Pali Ghar recently. They plan to build a road from the village to here, over the remains of the *Parmat Lain*!'

We were soon back in Chakanagar. Santosh borrowed a bicycle to go to the river crossing and collect Shabir and his *tonga*. I waited at the tea stall, graciously accepting the congratulations of the men who had previously assured us that the Customs Line was completely buried.

Raja came trotting at a brisk pace. It was getting dark, so I climbed up straight away and we were off. Santosh and Shabir talked with enthusiasm about our find. Santosh seemed not to realise that our search was finally over, and that he was about to return to an angry family. Once again, we crossed the Yamuna as the red sun was setting into it. On the other side of the river Raja settled into a faster stride, anxious to get home. As the sky darkened, I contemplated my success.

After three years of research and travel, I had found the remnants of the great hedge of India – the greatest hedge the world had ever known. All the sceptics, all those who doubted whether the Customs Hedge had really ever existed, had been proved wrong. It was true that I had not found very much in the way of remains, but I had long ago given up hope of finding mile upon mile of perfect hedge, like those clipped yew hedges of English stately homes. That had been what I had first dreamed of, as I had also dreamed of riding along the entire length in some romantic way – on a horse, or maybe a camel. I had long ago accepted that the reason no one knew of the hedge was precisely because it had largely disappeared. If it had been better preserved it would have become a tourist attraction.

Of course, it might be that I had failed to discover some longer, or more intact, section of the Customs Hedge. I could spend the rest of my life searching for more accurate maps; traipsing the vast spaces of India. It might be that an archival treasure-trove was waiting to be discovered. A cache of old photographs might provide startling new evidence. Eventually, satellite photographs might show every detail of the terrain. Detailed examination of the land records might reveal the exact path of the hedge. I was satisfied, however, with what I had found. It was time to give up my obsession; time to move on.

Over the past three years I had learnt something about India, and the Indians. I had learnt a good deal more about the British in India. When I had first started my search for the Customs Hedge, I had been looking for a folly, a harmless piece of English eccentricity. It had been a shock to find that the great hedge was in reality a monstrosity; a terrible instru-

ment of British oppression. Nevertheless, by then I was so obsessed with my quest that I had persevered. I had devoted all my spare time to the search; all my vacations; all my thoughts. Now, at last, I had accomplished my mission. It was over.

I knew I should have felt supremely happy. Yet I was rather sad. A melancholy had settled on me. As I pulled my shawl tighter against the chill air, a pair of nightjars flew aimlessly overhead. They churred plaintively.

Glossary

banghie	shoulder-mounted bamboo sling
bhar	a sack
chapati	flat bread
chowkey	customs post
dacoit	bandit
dal	lentils, or other pulses
dhoti	a man's long loincloth
factory	trading post
ghat (ghaut)	river landing place
ghee	clarified butter
ghurra	plank used as a boat seat
godown	warehouse
gunny	a sack
lassi	yoghurt thinned with water
-ji	respectful name suffix
lakh	a hundred thousand
lathi	heavy bamboo stick
lingam	phallic image of Lord Shiva
namaste	Hindi greeting
orni	a woman's head covering
pakora	chopped vegetables, etc, fried in spiced batter
panchayat	village council

paratha	fried flat bread
pargana	administrative district
roti	flat bread
ryot	peasant, cultivating tenant
salwar-kameez	woman's costume of loose trousers and blouse
sarpanch	chair of panchayat
tabla	a small drum
tilak	ornamental forehead mark
zamindar	major landowner

Weights and Measures
– APPROXIMATE EQUIVALENTS

One British Pound (Sterling) = 10 Indian Rupees
One Maund = 82 pounds weight = 37 kilograms
One Saggio = ⅙ ounce = 5 grams

Imperial	*Metric*
ounce	28 grams
pound	454 grams
ton	1,016 kilograms
foot	0.3 metre
yard	0.9 metre
mile	1.6 kilometres
pint	0.6 litre

Commas in large numbers are positioned in the British style.

The ⚖ used throughout this book appeared on some late-eighteenth- and early-nineteenth-century East India Company coins. Between the scales was written عدل, Adel, the Persian word for 'Justice'.

Select Bibliography

K. T. Achaya, *Indian Food: A Historical Companion* (Delhi: Oxford University Press, 1994)

S. C. Aggarwal, *The Salt Industry in India,* second edition (Delhi: Government Press, 1956)

Pramathanath Banerjea, *Indian Finance in the Days of the Company* (London: Macmillan, 1928)

Tarasankar Banerjee, *Internal Market of India, 1834–1900* (Calcutta: Academic Publishers, 1966)

Yves-Marie Berce, *Revolt and Revolution in Early Modern Europe,* trans. by Joseph Bergin (Manchester: Manchester University Press, 1987)

M. R. Bloch, 'The Social Influence of Salt', *Scientific American,* 209 (1963) 89–98

H. Bruce, *The Salt Sources of India and the Customs Preventive Establishment of the North-West Provinces, and the Punjab* (Calcutta: P. M. Craneburgh, 1863)

George Campbell, *Modern India: A Sketch of the System of Civil Government,* second edition (London: John Murray, 1853)

Samuel Couling, *The Encyclopaedia Sinica* (London: Humphrey Milford, 1917)

229

Abhay Charan Das, *The Indian Ryot: Land Tax, Permanent Settlement, and the Famine* (Howrah: Howrah Press, 1881)

Derek A. Denton, *The Hunger for Salt: An Anthropological, Physiological and Medical Analysis* (Berlin: Springer-Verlag, 1982)

Stephen Dowell, *A History of Taxation and Taxes in England* (London: Longmans, Green, 1888)

Uday Chand Dutt, *The Materia Medica of the Hindus* (Varanasi: Chowkhamba Saraswatibhawan, 1980)

J. Edkins, *The Revenue and Taxation of the Chinese Empire* (Shanghai: Presbyterian Mission Press, 1903)

Brij Gopal and K. P. Sharma, *Sambhar Lake: Rajasthan* (New Delhi: World Wide Fund for Nature, India, 1994)

M. S. Jain, *Concise History of Modern Rajasthan* (New Delhi: Wishwa Prakashan, 1993)

H. L. Marriott, *Water and Salt Depletion* (Springfield, Illinois: Charles C. Thomas, 1950)

Robert P. Multhauf, *Neptune's Gift; A History of Common Salt* (Baltimore: Johns Hopkins University Press, 1978)

Marco Polo, *The Travels of Marco Polo,* Everyman's Library edition (London: J. M. Dent, 1908)

Parimal Ray, 'History of Taxation under the Rule of the East India Company', *Calcutta Review,* ser 3, 33–7 (1929–30)

Knut Schmidt-Nielsen, *Desert Animals: Physiological Problems of Heat and Water* (Oxford: Clarendon Press, 1964)

W. H. Sleeman, *Rambles and Recollections of an Indian Official,* Constable's Oriental Miscellany edition, edited by Vincent Arthur Smith (London: Archibald Constable, 1893)

Select Bibliography

Sir John Strachey and Richard Strachey, *The Finances and Public Works of India, 1869–1881* (London: Kegan Paul, Trench, 1882)

C. E. Trevelyan, *Report upon the Inland Customs and Town Duties of the Bengal Presidency,* second edition (Calcutta: 1835)

Sir George Trevelyan, *The Competition Wallah,* second edition (London and New York: Macmillan, 1895)

Sir George Watt, *A Dictionary of the Economic Products of India* (Calcutta: Government Press; London: W. H. Allen, 1889–96)

Thomas Weber, *On the Salt March: The Historiography of Gandhi's March to Dandi* (New Delhi: HarperCollins, 1997)

Stanley A. Wolpert, *A New History of India* (New York: Oxford University Press, 1989)

B. D. Yadav, *A. O. Hume, 'Founder of Congress,* Indian Freedom Fighter Series – 32 (New Delhi: Anmol Publications, 1992)

OFFICIAL PUBLICATIONS

The Dictionary of National Biography, edited by Sir Leslie Stephen and Sir Sidney Lee (London: Oxford University Press, 1921–7)

District Gazetters of the United Provinces of Agra and Oudh, edited by H. R. Nevill (Allahabad: Government Press, 1903–36)

The East-India Register and Directory, continued as *The East-India Register and Army List, The Indian Army and Civil Service List,* and *The India List Civil and Military* (London: 1803–95)

The Imperial Gazetteer of India, edited by W. W. Hunter (London: Trubner, 1881)

Manual for the Guidance of Officers of the Excise and Salt Department (Calcutta: Bengal Secretariat Press, 1918)

Midnapore Salt Papers: Hijli and Tamluk, 1781–1807, edited by Narendra Krishna Sinha (Calcutta: West Bengal Regional Records Survey, 1954)

Monograph on Common Salt (Calcutta: Federation of Indian Chambers of Commerce and Industry, 1930)

Report on the Administration of the Inland Customs Department (Allahabad: Government Press, 1868–78)

Statistical Descriptive and Historical Account of the North-Western Provinces of India, edited by Edwin T. Atkinson and others (Allahabad: Government Press, 1874–86)

Parliamentary Papers: 'Report from the Select Committee on Salt, British India', 1836 (518) XVII

Parliamentary Papers: 'Report of the Commissioner appointed to Inquire into and Report upon the Manufacture and Sale of Salt in British India', 1856 (2084 I) XXVI

Parliamentary Papers: 'Report of the Indian Famine Commission, Part III, Famine Histories', 1881 (C 3086) LXXI – Part I

Acknowledgements

As the book makes clear, I am indebted to many people for their help, both in Britain and in India. Some I have mentioned by name, but I am grateful to many others. I particularly wish to thank my ever-cheerful companion on the search for the Customs Hedge, Santosh Kumar Nishad.

My researches in Britain were made much easier by the courtesies I received from the staff of the libraries at the Oriental and India Office Collections of the British Library, the Royal Geographical Society, the Natural History Museum, University College London, the School of African and Oriental Studies, and the Institute of Commonwealth Studies in the University of London. My colleagues at the University of London Library were very indulgent to a non-librarian, and gave me much assistance.

I am grateful to Kamlesh Aurora, Sangeet Atasa, and Sarfaraz Ahmad for persevering in the difficult task of teaching me a little Hindi, and to Rupert Snell for advice on some awkward translations.

My brother, John, helped me with his medical knowledge, and my niece, Maddy, with her confidence that I would find the Customs Hedge. Graham Keen assisted with the map. Angela Atkins and Maria Lord gave helpful advice on earlier drafts. Carol O'Brien, and her colleagues at Constable, made useful suggestions on how the book might be improved. Finally, Helen Armitage put in a great deal of editorial work, and corrected my English. I am very grateful to all these good friends.

233

Web Site and Feedback

Since completing this book, I have partly reconsidered my decision to end research into the Customs Hedge. It seemed a pity not to share any information readers might possess. A web site has been set up to facilitate this, and I hope readers will want to participate. I have put up some additional material myself. As well as more general history about the Customs Hedge, any information from old photographs or family records would be especially welcome. If suitable these could be posted on the site.

www.roymoxham.com

(e-mail: mail@roymoxham.com)